GLORIA
ESTEFAN

WOMEN OF ACHIEVEMENT

GLORIA ESTEFAN

Jane Phillips

CHELSEA HOUSE PUBLISHERS
PHILADELPHIA

Frontispiece: Gloria Estefan, shown holding her Grammy Award for Best Tropical Latin Performance in 1996, knows that her positive approach to life has helped her overcome tragedy and brought her stunning success.

PRODUCED BY 21st Century Publishing and Communications, Inc., New York, N.Y.

Chelsea House Publishers
EDITOR IN CHIEF Sally Cheney
ASSOCIATE EDITOR IN CHIEF Kim Shinners
PRODUCTION MANAGER Pamela Loos
ART DIRECTOR Sara Davis
DIRECTOR OF PHOTOGRAPHY Judy L. Hasday
COVER DESIGNER Keith Trego

The Chelsea House World Wide Web address is
http://www.chelseahouse.com

First Printing
1 3 5 7 9 8 6 4 2

Library of Congress Cataloging-in-Publication Data

Phillips, Jane.
Gloria Estefan / Jane Phillips.
   p. cm. — (Women of achievement)
Includes bibliographical references and index.
ISBN 0-7910-5883-2 (alk. paper) — ISBN 0-7910-5884-0 (pbk.: alk. paper)
1. Estefan, Gloria—Juvenile literature. 2. Singers—United States—
Biography—Juvenile literature. 3. Women singers—United States—
Biography—Juvenile literature. [1. Estefan, Gloria. 2. Singers.
3. Cuban Americans—Biography. 4. Women—Biography.] I. Title.
II. Series.

ML3930.E85 P55 2000
782.42164'092—dc21
[B]   00-060157

CONTENTS

WOMEN of ACHIEVEMENT

Jane Addams
SOCIAL WORKER

Madeleine Albright
STATESWOMAN

Marian Anderson
SINGER

Susan B. Anthony
WOMAN SUFFRAGIST

Clara Barton
AMERICAN RED CROSS FOUNDER

Margaret Bourke-White
PHOTOGRAPHER

Rachel Carson
BIOLOGIST AND AUTHOR

Cher
SINGER AND ACTRESS

Hillary Rodham Clinton
FIRST LADY AND ATTORNEY

Katie Couric
JOURNALIST

Diana, Princess of Wales
HUMANITARIAN

Emily Dickinson
POET

Elizabeth Dole
POLITICIAN

Amelia Earhart
AVIATOR

Gloria Estefan
SINGER

Jodie Foster
ACTRESS AND DIRECTOR

Betty Friedan
FEMINIST

Althea Gibson
TENNIS CHAMPION

Ruth Bader Ginsburg
SUPREME COURT JUSTICE

Helen Hayes
ACTRESS

Katharine Hepburn
ACTRESS

Mahalia Jackson
GOSPEL SINGER

Helen Keller
HUMANITARIAN

**Ann Landers/
Abigail Van Buren**
COLUMNISTS

Barbara McClintock
BIOLOGIST

Margaret Mead
ANTHROPOLOGIST

Edna St. Vincent Millay
POET

Julia Morgan
ARCHITECT

Toni Morrison
AUTHOR

Grandma Moses
PAINTER

Lucretia Mott
WOMAN SUFFRAGIST

Sandra Day O'Connor
SUPREME COURT JUSTICE

Rosie O'Donnell
ENTERTAINER AND COMEDIAN

Georgia O'Keeffe
PAINTER

Eleanor Roosevelt
DIPLOMAT AND HUMANITARIAN

Wilma Rudolph
CHAMPION ATHLETE

Elizabeth Cady Stanton
WOMAN SUFFRAGIST

Harriet Beecher Stowe
AUTHOR AND ABOLITIONIST

Barbra Streisand
ENTERTAINER

Elizabeth Taylor
ACTRESS AND ACTIVIST

Mother Teresa
HUMANITARIAN AND
RELIGIOUS LEADER

Barbara Walters
JOURNALIST

Edith Wharton
AUTHOR

Phillis Wheatley
POET

Oprah Winfrey
ENTERTAINER

Babe Didrikson Zaharias
CHAMPION ATHLETE

"REMEMBER THE LADIES"

MATINA S. HORNER

"Remember the Ladies." That is what Abigail Adams wrote to her husband John, then a delegate to the Continental Congress, as the Founding Fathers met in Philadelphia to form a new nation in March of 1776. "Be more generous and favorable to them than your ancestors. Do not put such unlimited power in the hands of the Husbands. If particular care and attention is not paid to the Ladies," Abigail Adams warned, "we are determined to foment a Rebellion, and will not hold ourselves bound by any Laws in which we have no voice, or Representation."

The words of Abigail Adams, one of the earliest American advocates of women's rights, were prophetic. Because when we have not "remembered the ladies," they have, by their words and deeds, reminded us so forcefully of the omission that we cannot fail to remember them. For the history of American women is as interesting and varied as the history of our nation as a whole. American women have played an integral part in founding, settling, and building our country. Some we remember as remarkable women who—against great odds—achieved distinction in the public arena: Anne Hutchinson, who in the 17th century became a charismatic

7

religious leader; Phillis Wheatley, an 18th-century black slave who became a poet; Susan B. Anthony, whose name is synonymous with the 19th-century women's rights movement, and who led the struggle to enfranchise women; and in the 20th century, Amelia Earhart, the first woman to cross the Atlantic Ocean by air.

These extraordinary women certainly merit our admiration, but other women, "common women," many of them all but forgotten, should also be recognized for their contributions to American thought and culture. Women have been community builders; they have founded schools and formed voluntary associations to help those in need; they have assumed the major responsibility for rearing children, passing on from one generation to the next the values that keep a culture alive. These and innumerable other contributions, once ignored, are now being recognized by scholars, students, and the public. It is exciting and gratifying that a part of our history that was hardly acknowledged a few generations ago is now being studied and brought to light.

In recent decades, the field of women's history has grown from obscurity to a politically controversial splinter movement to academic respectability, in many cases mainstreamed into such traditional disciplines as history, economics, and psychology. Scholars of women, both female and male, have organized research centers at such prestigious institutions as Wellesley College, Stanford University, and the University of California. Other notable centers for women's studies are the Center for the American Woman and Politics at the Eagleton Institute of Politics at Rutgers University; the Henry A. Murray Research Center for the Study of Lives, at Radcliffe College; and the Women's Research and Education Institute, the research arm of the Congressional Caucus on Women's Issues. Other scholars and public figures have established archives and libraries, such as the Schlesinger Library on the History of Women in America, at Radcliffe College, and the Sophia Smith Collection, at Smith College, to collect and preserve the written and tangible legacies of women.

From the initial donation of the Women's Rights Collection in 1943, the Schlesinger Library grew to encompass vast collections documenting the manifold accomplishments of American women. Simultaneously, the women's movement in general and the academic discipline of women's studies in particular also began with a narrow definition and gradually expanded their mandate. Early causes, such as woman suffrage and social reform, abolition, and organized labor were joined by newer concerns, such as the history of women in business and the professions and in politics and government; the study of the family; and social issues such as health policy and education.

Women, as historian Arthur M. Schlesinger, jr., once pointed out, "have constituted the most spectacular casualty of traditional history. They have made up at least half the human race, but you could never tell that by looking at the books historians write." The new breed of historians is remedying that omission. They have written books about immigrant women and about working-class women who struggled for survival in cities and about black women who met the challenges of life in rural areas. They are telling the stories of women who, despite the barriers of tradition and economics, became lawyers and doctors and public figures.

The women's studies movement has also led scholars to question traditional interpretations of their respective disciplines. For example, the study of war has traditionally been an exercise in military and political analysis, an examination of strategies planned and executed by men. But scholars of women's history have pointed out that wars have also been periods of tremendous change and even opportunity for women, because the very absence of men on the home front enabled them to expand their educational, economic, and professional activities and to assume leadership in their homes.

The early scholars of women's history showed a unique brand of courage in choosing to investigate new subjects and take new approaches to old ones. Often, like their subjects, they endured criticism and even ostracism by their academic colleagues. But their efforts have unquestionably been worthwhile, because with the publication of each new study and book another piece of the historical patchwork is sewn into place, revealing an increasingly comprehensive picture of the role of women in our rich and varied history.

Such books on groups of women are essential, but books that focus on the lives of individuals are equally indispensable. Biographies can be inspirational, offering their readers the example of people with vision who have looked outside themselves for their goals and have often struggled against great obstacles to achieve them. Marian Anderson, for instance, had to overcome racial bigotry in order to perfect her art and perform as a concert singer. Isadora Duncan defied the rules of classical dance to find true artistic freedom. Jane Addams had to break down society's notions of the proper role for women in order to create new social situations, notably the settlement house. All of these women had to come to terms both with themselves and with the world in which they lived. Only then could they move ahead as pioneers in their chosen callings.

Biography can inspire not only by adulation but also by realism. It helps us to see not only the qualities in others that we hope to emulate, but also, perhaps, the weaknesses that made them "human." By helping us identify with the subject on a more personal level they help us feel that we, too, can achieve such goals. We read about Eleanor Roosevelt, for instance, who occupied a unique and seemingly enviable position as the wife of the president. Yet we can sympathize with her inner dilemma; an inherently shy woman, she had to force herself to live a most public life in order to use her position to benefit others. We may not be able to imagine ourselves having the immense poetic talent of Emily Dickinson, but from her story we can understand the challenges faced by a creative woman who was expected to fulfill many family responsibilities. And though few of us will ever reach the level of athletic accomplishment displayed by Wilma Rudolph or Babe Zaharias, we can still appreciate their spirit, their overwhelming will to excel.

A biography is a multifaceted lens. It is first of all a magnification, the intimate examination of one particular life. But at the same time, it is a wide-angle lens, informing us about the world in which the subject lived. We come away from reading about one life knowing more about the social, political, and economic fabric of the time. It is for this reason, perhaps, that the great New England essayist Ralph Waldo Emerson wrote in 1841, "There is properly no history: only biography." And it is also why biography, and particularly women's biography, will continue to fascinate writers and readers alike.

With husband Emilio, Gloria Estefan enjoys the joys of a dazzling music career and a devoted family life that was highlighted in 1994 with the birth of their daughter, Emily.

1

ON TOP OF THE WORLD

Gloria Estefan counted her blessings as she looked down at the beautiful baby girl who had finally appeared in her life. Her new daughter, Emily, born on December 5, 1994, looked just like her—so sweet and shy. Gloria had traveled a long way to reach this point, and the musical superstar knew that she had much to be thankful for.

Gloria Estefan's rich, full life includes a loving husband (who is also her business partner), a family, and a sizzling musical career. Since she and her backup band, the Miami Sound Machine, broke onto the pop music scene in the early 1980s, Gloria has sold more than 70 million records worldwide. She is still going strong. In 2000 she was nominated for three Grammy Awards, earned the Award of Merit honor at the American Music Awards, and won a Latin Grammy Award for Best Music Video ("No Me Dejes de Querer"). Her concerts consistently sell out and feature spectacular, high-energy performances of her fast-paced songs as well as slow, touching deliveries of her popular ballads.

Dubbed the Queen of Latin Pop and the Latin Diva, Gloria has

contributed significantly to the current popularity of
Latin music in the United States by breaking down
the musical barriers between Spanish- and English-
speaking artists. In doing so, she has forged a path for
today's up-and-coming Latino talents, including
Ricky Martin, Shakira, Julieta Venegas, Cassia Eller,
Jon Secada, and Andrea Echeverri. Gloria was one of
the first Latin "crossover" artists, meaning that her
music became popular not only among pop music
fans but also among fans of dance and soft rock. Her
first hit song, "Conga," made her the first artist ever
to land a place on *Billboard*'s Pop, Dance, Black, and
Latin charts at the same time.

Gloria is especially loved by her fellow Cuban
Americans. Fans say she is sweet and kind—always
willing to sign autographs—and that she displays
genuine concern for those less fortunate than she.
Gloria and her husband, Emilio, are well known for
their generous contributions to charities and for their
willingness to help raise money for those who have
survived natural disasters. They both understand what
it is like to be extremely poor and to struggle through
difficult times. They realize that their success allows
them to contribute to the Latin American community
in ways that most people cannot.

The Estefans can afford to be generous: Gloria and
Emilio have been listed together by the business journal
Forbes as the world's 31st richest entertainers. Their
financial worth is conservatively valued at more than
$200 million. This monetary success is due not only to
Gloria's wonderful voice and performing abilities but
also to Emilio's business sense and his instincts about
musical trends. The couple owns Estefan Enterprises,
an enormous company with varied business interests,
including a number of hotels and many Spanish restaurants such as the Bongo Cuban Café at Disney World
in Florida. One of Estefan Enterprises' most notable
businesses, however, is Crescent Moon Recording Studio

in Miami. Musical superstars such as Madonna, Céline Dion, Clarence Clemons, Aerosmith, and the Rolling Stones, along with many new Latin musicians, have gone to the studio to spice up their music with a Latin beat.

Emilio Estefan has been called the Godfather of Latin Pop. He has been compared to Berry Gordy, the powerhouse who launched the Motown record label and brought fame to dozens of African-American acts during the 1960s and 1970s. For decades Emilio has mentored aspiring Latino artists by helping to bring their music into the mainstream and by introducing them to audiences around the world. He did much the same with Gloria when she was just starting out in the music field. Without the couple's influence, today's Latin music would be vastly different.

Gloria has been especially inspirational for the

By breaking down barriers between Spanish- and English-speaking artists, Gloria forged a path for younger Latino performers such as Ricky Martin. Here Gloria and Ricky perform with Celia Cruz (left) at the First Annual Latin Grammy Awards held in Los Angeles on September 13, 2000.

current crop of female Latin—or Latina—artists (dubbed *rockeras)* from countries such as Mexico, Puerto Rico, Colombia, Brazil, and Cuba. Women still have a tough time breaking into the "macho" world of Latin music, which traditionally has been characterized by all-male bands and male vocalists. Before Gloria appeared on the scene, many Latin American women found places as backup singers, but they rarely ended up on center stage. Today's Latina artists find it easier to break through, and they are well aware of the debt they owe to Gloria Estefan.

Gloria herself is quick to credit Emilio's hard work. The couple were the first entertainers to fuse Latin and disco beats with the English language—a combination that Emilio calls "a cross between rice, beans, and hamburger." They created a new, fresh, and very likable sound that has endured several decades of musical revolution in the United States and is evident in today's Latin pop music. "I think what happened with [rhythm-and-blues] at Motown is what's happening with Latin music now," Emilio told *Time* magazine in 1999. "It's like a sleeping giant waking up all over the world."

In Miami's Cuban community, Gloria is affection-ately called "Nuestra Glorita" (our little Gloria). It's easy to see why the Estefans are so greatly admired by their fellow Cuban Americans. They are hardworking people with strong family ties, and they hold values shared by the rest of the community. They also remain free of scandal—a difficult feat for public figures watched by millions of fans.

Although their values are firmly grounded, Gloria's music constantly changes. She likes to keep fans on their toes. On some of her albums she gives the impression of being fragile or melancholy; on others she is loving and expansive. Her 1998 album, *gloria!,* shows fans that she is also a dramatic diva with an intoxicating sense of soul.

Emilio and Gloria were the first entertainers to fuse Latin and disco beats with the English language. Emilio compares Latin music to "a sleeping giant waking up all over the world."

Adoring fans surround the artist as she launches her album gloria! *during a party at New York City's Studio 54 on May 29, 1998.*

The Estefans have obtained the American dream— but they have not always led such comfortable lives. Their success has not come easily. Gloria especially has experienced many struggles and tragedies. She survived a sad and turbulent childhood as a Cuban immigrant in Miami. She has recovered from a broken back, caused when a tractor trailer hit her tour bus. Rifts between the Estefans and their band and family members marked Gloria's climb to superstardom. She and Emilio have their share of former friends to whom they no longer speak.

Throughout her trials, however, Gloria Estefan continues to maintain a bright outlook on life, and she is a firm believer in the power of positive thinking. She believes that we can all accomplish great things if we set our minds to doing so and remain focused on our goals. Gloria herself is driven to succeed—and she has battled great odds on her way to stardom.

Gloria María with her mother, Gloria Fajardo. The baby was born into a comfortably well-off Cuban family, but tumultuous political events soon transformed the Fajardos' lives.

2

A LONELY CHILDHOOD

When Gloria María Fajardo was born in the capital city of Havana, Cuba, on September 1, 1957, her parents were thrilled. But not all was well on the island nation. Cuba's ruler, President Fulgencio Batista y Zaldívar (called "Batista"), was a controversial leader. Many Cubans disliked and distrusted Batista because he was corrupt. A great number of citizens suffered while he led the country. Afraid that they might try to overthrow him, Batista suppressed free speech and freedom of the press to keep tight control over his people.

The Cubans who supported Batista were called Batistianos. They believed that he offered them power and wealth. The U.S. government helped Batista's regime as well. It didn't like all his policies, but in its view, at least Batista was not a communist. The United States believed that it was important for communism to be kept out of nations, especially those close to North America.

At the time Gloria was born, an anti-Batista movement was rumbling across Cuba. One of its leaders was a lawyer named Fidel Castro. He supported communist ideas. The United States was worried that Castro might become Cuba's leader and bring communism to a nation only 90 miles south of Florida.

In spite of these political tensions, wealthy and middle-class Americans continued to flock to Havana, a glamorous city with an exotic atmoshpere that appealed to vacationers. In the United States, Cuban goods such as hand-rolled cigars were in great demand, and anything with a Cuban flavor—music, dance, food, even little dogs—enjoyed broad popularity. Havana was home to Cuba's urban middle class, who lived comfortable lives. They benefited from both American tourists and exports to the United States.

Gloria's family was among those who were doing well in Havana. Her mother, also named Gloria, was a schoolteacher. Her father, José, was a security guard for President Batista's family. Cuba's political unrest made Batista and his followers very cautious, and José Fajardo was responsible for providing a motorcycle escort for Batista's wife, Marta Fernández de Batista, whenever she made trips by car through the city.

A strong, athletic man, José was a good choice for the job. He had been a member of the Cuban national volleyball team, which had won a medal at the Pan American Games (a kind of Olympics for North and South America). His immense size made Señora Batista feel secure, despite rumors of a government overthrow by Fidel Castro and his supporters.

In person, Fidel Castro was a charming man, and he had lofty political ambitions. Many Cubans who felt repressed under Batista's rule began to believe that Castro could help set their country free. They thought Castro would establish a powerful government under which they would prosper. During the late 1950s, as Castro's movement grew stronger, the two political factions clashed. Armed battles became common.

These conflicts reached a climax on January 1, 1959. Fidel Castro began the year by toppling the Batista government. Anticipating the coup, many of Cuba's wealthy residents—who had thrived under Batista's rule—fled the country the night before by boarding planes bound for Miami, Florida. Many of them left for the United States after attending New Year's Eve parties in Cuba, and they arrived in Florida still dressed in gowns and tuxedos, having abandoned their homes and possessions.

However, the people who had supported Batista and still remained in Cuba were in great danger. Many of them were rounded up and imprisoned.

José Fajardo realized that he had to get his family out of Cuba. While he had not been a major figure in the Batista government, it would only be a matter of time before he was imprisoned because of the work he had done for the Batista family. For several months, he was

In the 1950s, Americans loved the glamour and excitement of Havana, Cuba (above). Thousands of tourists vacationed in the "old world" city located just 60 miles away from the U.S. mainland.

unable to leave Cuba. Finally, late in 1959 the Fajardo family boarded a Pan American Airways jet bound for the United States. The family had round-trip tickets, purchased for about $20 each. Like most Cubans, they expected to be able to return to their native country after a short time. They kept their return plane tickets so that they would be ready to leave the United States as soon as Castro lost power.

One of the reasons the Fajardos and other Cuban refugees continued to hope that they would be able to return home soon was that the U.S. government was paying special attention to the changes taking place in Cuba. President Dwight D. Eisenhower, his administration, and the Central Intelligence Agency (CIA) were greatly concerned about the situation because Cuba was so close to the United States. If communism took hold and Cuba built strong ties to the communist government of the Soviet Union, the United States could be in danger. Later, some U.S. officials would worry that the Soviet Union might use Cuba as a base for missiles aimed at U.S. cities. The Cuban refugees believed that Castro wouldn't be able to stay in power if the United States decided to oppose him.

Most of the thousands of Cuban immigrants who fled to the United States after Castro took power in 1959 settled in the area around Miami. The city's temperate climate and warm ocean breezes reminded Cubans of their own country, and it was about as close to their homeland as they could get while remaining in the United States.

Cuban neighborhoods began to pop up in an area of Miami that came to be known as "Little Havana." The area quickly began to resemble Cuba, and the same types of shops and restaurants sprang up along streets filled with Cuban men talking about politics as they smoked cigars and drank strong, Cuban-style coffee. Cuban radio stations emerged, and Cuban music floated over the streets. The local restaurants

served traditional Cuban food, including a favorite spicy beef stew called *ropa vieja* (Spanish for "old clothes"). The major street in the new settlement, Calle Ocho, or Eighth Street, was crowded with Cubans who sought to escape their small, cramped apartments.

When the Fajardos arrived in America, they found an apartment in a run-down neighborhood near the Orange Bowl Stadium. The buildings were shabby, but they had been painted bright tropical colors. Still, the Fajardos' apartment was cold and dirty. Two-year-old

Gloria and her parents, having no beds or mattresses, slept on layers of newspapers to try to avoid the cold floor. They had left nearly all of their possessions behind when they fled Cuba.

For a family that had prospered in their homeland, the situation was difficult to handle. Years later, Gloria explained that starting over almost from nothing in an effort to live in freedom gives people a special perspective on life. "It's the immigrant mentality. . . . All of a sudden, boom, you're here," she has said. "You have nothing. It's hard to get rid of that feeling." Despite their desperate situation, Gloria's parents remained upbeat—a trait they passed on to their young daughter.

In spite of their efforts to be positive, the Fajardos could not ignore the disturbing news slowly reaching the Cuban community in Florida. Castro had seized the property and money that the Batistianos had left behind. Their homes and businesses were now government property. Even if the Cuban refugees could return to their homeland, life in Cuba would never be the same.

A great number of the Batistianos who remained in Cuba had been tortured and killed by Castro, and many of the Cuban refugees in America began to gather in groups to discuss ways of overthrowing the new Cuban leader. The refugees worked to gain sympathy for their cause. They wanted to persuade the U.S. government to bring Castro to justice. They had lost businesses, property, and in some cases family members in Cuba. They felt betrayed by their country and were angered over the injustices they had endured.

The Cuban refugees gained an important ally in the U.S. government. In 1960 President Dwight D. Eisenhower and the CIA developed plans to take action against the new Cuban regime and remove Fidel Castro from power. That would weaken or eliminate Cuba's ties with the Soviet Union. Some advisors suggested assassinating Castro. But the United States eventually decided to train and organize a force of Cuban exiles to invade the island. Because the invading troops would not be U.S. soldiers, the American government hoped to avoid the appearance of direct intervention. The plan was to take Castro by surprise and end his rule by weakening and destroying his army. Such action would allow another ruler—preferably a noncommunist —to take power.

Because the Batistianos in Florida believed that this action would clear the way for them to return home, they gladly volunteered for the mission, offering their complete support. The American government recruited about 1,500 of them and organized a small military unit. The men trained in Guatemala, then were sent to Nicaragua to await orders.

When her father left Miami to battle Castro in Cuba, Gloria remained behind, where she spent her early years in childhood play. Here, she poses in her cowboy outfit for a family photo.

Three-year-old Gloria and her mother stayed in their small apartment while José left Florida to train for the invasion. He knew how to operate a tank, but he wasn't familiar with the type of tank he was assigned to. That was just the beginning of his problems. The tank's radio didn't work, and its guns were stuck so he could not aim or shoot accurately.

His situation was not unusual. Many of the refugee soldiers were nervous and uncertain about whether they were properly prepared for their mission. They were working with outdated, worn equipment provided by the United States. Much of it dated from World War II or the Korean War.

Meanwhile Miami's Cuban neighborhoods were

full of tension. Almost all the men were gone. The immigrant women—most of whom spoke little or no English—banded together for support, sharing cars, food, clothing, jobs, and music. Gloria's mother knew that she needed to be strong while her husband was absent. Although the U.S. government gave small amounts of money to the wives of the Cuban refugee soldiers, the families still struggled. The women did their best to keep their children fed and clothed. Neighbors encouraged each other with reminders that the invasion would be brief and that their men would return to the United States quickly and triumphantly. Then they could return to Cuba.

On April 17, 1961, soon after the inauguration of John F. Kennedy, the invasion took place. It became known as the Bay of Pigs invasion after Bahía de los Cochinos, the bay where the refugees landed. José and the other soldiers succeeded at making a surprise landing on the Cuban coast, but they faced a well-equipped army that was ready for battle.

The fighting lasted only a day, but it was bloody and chaotic. Both forces were made up of Cubans, so it was hard to know who was fighting for the refugees and who was fighting for Castro. Communications with the United States were so bad that even when some of Castro's soldiers surrendered, the refugee soldiers had no idea what to do with their prisoners. Without any direction, the invading troops were forced to make their own decisions during battle.

However, only a few of Castro's forces surrendered. With their superior equipment, they quickly gained the upper hand. Many of the refugee soldiers were killed or captured. It was later learned that during the last hours of the invasion, the United States realized it had made a terrible mistake and began to back out of the operation. It stopped bombing Castro's air force and discontinued dropping off ammunition for the refugee soldiers on the ground,

Cuban exiles captured during the Bay of Pigs invasion in April 1961 walk past Fidel Castro's soldiers. Gloria's father was also captured, and he did not see his family for more than a year.

leaving them stranded and facing Castro's forces alone on the Cuban coast.

The refugees realized too late what had happened. They were in deep trouble. U.S. planes and ships were not coming back for them. They had been left behind without support. To avoid being captured, some of them tried to disappear into the jungle, but they were discovered by Castro's army and held captive for the next year and a half in prisons throughout Cuba.

Gloria's father was one of the soldiers who attempted to escape into the jungle. He had been wounded in the fighting, although not seriously. After many days, he was captured and imprisoned in Havana. Conditions

Fidel Castro's compelling speeches helped him develop a loyal following among Cuban citizens.

The Cuban Missile Crisis

After the failed Bay of Pigs invasion in April 1961, the U.S. government still worried about the situation in Cuba. Fidel Castro remained Cuba's leader, and he had close ties to the Soviet Union. Nikita Khrushchev, the leader of the Soviet Union, had promised to defend Cuba with Soviet arms. American leaders were concerned that these arms might include nuclear weapons.

The U.S. military sent U-2 spy planes over Cuba to discover what was happening on the island nation. In July 1962, those fears were confirmed. The United States learned that the Soviet Union was shipping missiles to Cuba. In August, the U-2 spy plane pilots took photos that showed new military construction. Photos taken on October 14 provided evidence of a ballistic missile launching site.

President Kennedy positioned U.S. ships so that they would block Cuba from receiving shipments of missiles from the Soviet Union. He announced the blockade on October 22. The president warned that U.S. forces would seize any "offensive weapons and associated material" that Soviet ships tried to deliver to Cuba. Many people were convinced that the United States and the Soviet Union were about to start a nuclear war.

Nikita Khrushchev and President Kennedy exchanged several messages about the tense situation. Six days later, on October 28, 1962, Khrushchev agreed to stop the work on the missile sites in Cuba and return all the missiles to the Soviet Union. The United States promised never again to invade Cuba. The crisis was over by the end of November, and the next month, prisoners from the Bay of Pigs invasion began to return to the United States.

were bad, but his concerned family could not learn anything about him. Although Gloria's mother made numerous attempts to send mail to him, all her letters were returned. The American-Cuban History Museum in Little Havana contains one of those letters. It had been returned by the Cuban government with a statement that Cuba had no prisoners of war.

Little Gloria mourned her father's absence. At first her mother tried to keep the news of his imprisonment from the little girl, but Gloria eventually overheard neighbors talking about the men of their community being held in Cuba. A sense of sadness spread throughout the Cuban community. Many of the women tried to remain brave, but without the emotional and financial support of their husbands, fathers, brothers, and sons, they soon became destitute.

Castro eventually demanded that the United States pay him a ransom of $62 million for the return of the refugee prisoners. Many Americans, who felt that the Bay of Pigs invasion had been a disaster, believed that the United States should take responsibility for the prisoners' welfare. Eventually, the U.S. government paid Castro $53 million in food and medicine to have the prisoners released. The men began to return to America late in December 1962. Some survivors were not released until July 1965.

José Fajardo's return to his family was bittersweet. Although Gloria and her mother were excited to have him home, he was now unemployed. However, José soon found work, joining the U.S. Army as an officer in 1963. The Fajardos moved to South Carolina and later to Texas.

During her years in South Carolina, living in a military family, Gloria had begun to realize that she lived an unusual life, although her parents tried very hard to build a "normal" home for her. When she begged them for a pet, it was hard to refuse, as Gloria explained:

While Gloria's father was away from home for long periods of time, she frequently wrote him letters and sometimes sent him audiotapes of songs she had recorded.

I have always had a great love for animals, but because my family was constantly uprooted due to my father's career in the Army, I was not allowed to have a pet. Then my dad was stationed in Fort Jackson, in Columbia, South Carolina, where we would be for at least two years. I began to campaign for a puppy, but my mom wasn't sure that I was mature enough at age nine to take care of a puppy myself. She finally told me that if I got straight A's on my report card she would consider getting me a dog. Well, I've always loved a challenge and came through on my part of the bargain. This is where my favorite childhood memory was born. We drove out to a farm where one of my dad's friends had a litter of German shepherd puppies. I knelt down on the ground, and one of the chubby, furry little pups ran right into my arms. I picked her up and she started licking my face, and I caught my first whiff of her irresistible puppy breath. Needless to say I was ecstatic and didn't put her down until we got home. I named her Dolly, and she was my best friend for years to come!

After José completed basic training, he was commissioned as an officer and then sent to Vietnam. Once again, little Gloria and her mother said good-bye to José. When her father left for the invasion of Cuba, Gloria had been too young to understand what was happening. But when her father was sent to Vietnam, she was old enough to know that he was in danger. She grew very worried and wrote letters to him frequently.

During those difficult years, Gloria began to discover her love of music. When the family lived in Florida, she had listened mainly to Miami's Spanish music stations, which played Cuban songs. But as her family moved to other areas of the country, she became exposed to American music. She loved listening to the songs of Johnny Mathis, Barbra Streisand, and Karen Carpenter. To ease the sadness she felt over her father's absence, Gloria began to spend hours alone in her room, singing and playing her guitar. She especially loved the sad ballads that she heard on American radio, and soon she began relying on the music she heard to lift her spirits.

Sometimes she sent her father audiotapes on which she had recorded herself speaking and singing. José wrote back and told his daughter that she was going to be a big star one day, a famous singer. He played Gloria's tapes for his fellow soldiers, and they all agreed that the little girl had great potential and a bright future.

Gloria's father returned home from Vietnam in 1968 and seemed to be unharmed by his wartime experiences. The following year, the Fajardos welcomed another daughter, Rebecca, into the family. Eleven-year-old Gloria had a baby sister. Life began to return to normal, and the family decided to move back to Miami where they could be close to other relatives. Though the Fajardos still struggled financially in Miami, José finally got a job and had a regular income.

Over the next few years, however, José began to

grow ill. Gloria remembers occasions when her father would be walking and suddenly fall. The strong father Gloria had always known became a weak man. He grew thin and pale, and his face became puffy.

Gloria and her mother both realized that something was terribly wrong with José, but they had no idea what it could be. Finally José saw a military doctor, who tentatively diagnosed him with a devastating disease known as multiple sclerosis (MS). MS affects physical coordination, and it grows progressively worse until the patient is unable to walk and has great difficulty talking. There is no cure, and many MS patients die from the condition.

But as the Fajardos later discovered, there may have been another explanation for José's symptoms. During the Vietnam War he and many other veterans had been exposed to a chemical mixture called Agent Orange. It had been used during the war by the United States to defoliate the trees and plants of Vietnamese jungles. By stripping the leaves from trees soldiers and pilots could easily spot the enemy.

Agent Orange was very toxic—not only for plants but for humans as well. Many Vietnam War veterans who have developed cancer and other diseases since the war blame their illnesses on their exposure to the substance, and a great number of medical doctors agree. In the early 1970s some military doctors simply diagnosed Vietnam veterans with symptoms similar to José's as having MS. It is not known if there is a link between José Fajardo's exposure to Agent Orange and his symptoms, but to this day Gloria Estefan and her mother believe that the chemical mixture caused his illness.

Initially, Gloria's mother cared for José. But because he could no longer work, the family did not have any income. Gloria's mother had to find a job to support her husband and children. At first she took any kind of work she could find and supported the family on her

In the early 1970s, Gloria assumed the responsibility of helping to care for her seriously ill father. When she found the time, Gloria found solace in music. "I sang instead of crying," she said.

salary. Gloria, by then a teenager, began caring for her father. Each day, she hurried home from school to sit with her dad and watch after her little sister, while her mother was at work. Years later, drawing on her teaching experience in Cuba, Gloria's mother became qualified to teach school in the United States.

The responsibilities of caring for the family forced Gloria to grow up quickly. She remembers this time as a painful period of her life: "I felt really alone in my life," she's said. "It was a situation that I could see no way of getting out of." Every day, Gloria had to feed and bathe her father. As time passed, it became clear that Gloria's father needed full-time

Gloria poses for her first communion—one of the most important religious events of her childhood.

nursing care, but the family could not afford it. So in the strong Cuban tradition, they shouldered the responsibility themselves.

And that responsibility was growing. José began showing signs of losing his memory. At first he would forget what he was doing in the middle of a task. Eventually his memory of past events began to fade. "My father would stand up, forget he couldn't walk and fall down," Gloria explained in an interview. "I had to pick him up a lot, and he felt bad about that."

Though his illness was not his fault, José felt

ashamed of having placed such a burden on his family. He was embarrassed to have his daughter take care of him, and this knowledge made Gloria feel even more isolated. She has said that she watched her father fade and die over many years.

Gloria was also experiencing the confusion and self-consciousness of growing up. Her only relief during this period came from her music. "When I was a teenager, I was fat, I was shy, I wore glasses, I had [big eyebrows] and hair all over my body," she recalled. "They were years of torture. It was very depressing and scary for me. Music was the one bright spot in my life. My child-hood made me very serious and introverted; music was an escape from that. I sang instead of crying."

Gloria soon realized that the only time she didn't feel shy was when she was singing. She wrote sad ballads, which she performed for her family and neighbors despite her shyness. All agreed that she had a beautiful voice. During these difficult years, Gloria spent more and more time immersed in music.

And Gloria loved singing. As a student at Our Lady of Lourdes Girls Parochial School, she and her cousin Merci sang and played guitar in a number of school concerts and recitals. They were quite good, and the other students and their parents loved to hear the two teenage girls. Neither Gloria nor her cousin planned on a musical career. They were content to perform before small groups of appreciative friends and family mem-bers. Sometimes Gloria thought about starting a band of her own, but for the moment, she continued to use music as a way to express her feelings about the difficult situation with her father.

When Gloria was 16 years old, her father was placed in a Veterans Administration hospital. He never came home again. For years, Gloria visited her dad in the hospital, watching his mind and body deteriorate. But it wasn't long before another important man entered her life.

Initially skeptical of Emilio's charms, Gloria eventually realized that there was something about Emilio that made her want to spend the rest of her life with him.

3

SOMETHING ABOUT EMILIO

Gloria first saw Emilio Estefan when he came to her school to speak to music students about what it was like to have a band. He had founded the Miami Latin Boys, a local group that was popular among Cuban immigrants. Gloria didn't speak to Emilio at the time, but she remembered thinking how handsome he was.

At the time, Emilio had a full-time job at Bacardi Imports, a Puerto Rican distiller and rum distributor. One of his coworkers had a son who was a friend of Gloria's. The man wanted his son to start a band and thought Gloria and her cousin should join too. Emilio was invited to the man's home. "The first time I met Emilio was at a mutual friend's house," Gloria recalled. "They called him over because he had the Miami Latin Boys together and he was going to give us some pointers on how to get a band together to do a show for one night, just for fun."

Emilio noted that Gloria was beautiful in an innocent sort of way but that she also seemed to have been through a lot. Gloria sang for Emilio at that meeting, but she got the feeling that he wasn't very impressed.

Gloria didn't expect to see Emilio again—and she wouldn't have if her mother hadn't talked her into attending the wedding of a friend's daughter. Gloria really didn't want to go because she didn't know the bride very well. But she agreed to accompany her mother so the older woman wouldn't have to attend alone. At the reception, Gloria was surprised to see the Miami Latin Boys had been hired to provide the music. She had never actually seen Emilio perform, and she was impressed with his wild style. He seemed to be having fun and didn't appear to mind if he made a bit of a fool of himself. He had a lot of energy and pizzazz, and the guests loved him.

Gloria admired Emilio's outgoing nature, and she was mesmerized by this good-looking clown. When Emilio spotted Gloria, he recognized her from his friend's house. During a break, he came to her table and asked whether she would come up and sing a few songs with the band. Gloria gave him an adamant no, but her mother insisted that she sing.

It seemed that the band didn't want Gloria on stage either, which made her feel even more shy and awkward than usual. They didn't want to hear an amateur do a terrible job, and they didn't want to try to make her sound professional if she wasn't. Emilio, however, knew that Gloria wasn't going to do badly because he had already heard her sing and thought she was pretty good. He insisted that the band members relax and enjoy the next few songs they played.

Reluctantly, Gloria went up on stage and sang two popular Cuban tunes. Once she got going, she had the whole room dancing. Emilio was extremely impressed with her performance—and so was the rest of the band. She was good! They convinced her to sing a couple more songs, and she left the stage, in shock, to a standing ovation.

Instantly the wheels started to turn in Emilio's mind. He realized that Gloria could be a great addition to the

When Emilio Estefan (front row, center) asked Gloria (second from left, standing) and her cousin Merci (right) to join the Miami Latin Boys, he broke with the tradition that Cuban bands feature male soloists.

Miami Latin Boys, and he wasn't going to let her get away. His band was in need of a lead singer. Why not hire this teenage girl? Although Cuban bands at the time used male soloists, Emilio had always been a free-thinking musician, and he was sure that a woman vocalist would not only make his band memorable but also make him famous.

Like Gloria, Emilio had been born in Cuba, but his life had greatly differed from hers. He had grown up near Guantanamo Bay, a region far from Havana. As a young child, his parents gave him an accordion, and he began to perform in a small band with other children. (Despite his great talent for music, Emilio never learned to read music. Instead, he plays everything by ear, learning and creating as he goes.) At age 12, Emilio left for Spain with his father, so that the boy would not have to serve a mandatory stint in the Cuban army. His older brother was already required to serve and stayed behind with their mother.

Emilio's father was not a Batistiano like Gloria's father. But he did not support Fidel Castro, either. He refused to see his second son serve in the communist dictator's army. In Spain, however, Emilio and his father faced serious problems. The older man could not find a job, and the two went hungry many nights. Emilio has recalled that they had to turn to soup kitchens and shelters for their meals. After a time, Emilio found a job playing his accordion in a local restaurant. Father and son lived on Emilio's meager income, but the young man earned more than money. He earned self-respect, learning that he could support himself with his personality, spunk, and style.

Emilio and his father eventually left Spain for Miami, where Emilio got a student visa that allowed him to attend school. Emilio liked Miami, and he began to meet people and make friends. At age 16, he took a job in the mail room of Bacardi Imports while attending high school classes at night. With his engaging personality he soon befriended many coworkers, including upper-level managers who would later provide worthwhile business connections.

Emilio bought a bigger accordion and began performing in Miami restaurants. Then, with his friend Raul Murciano, he founded the Miami Latin Boys. Just for fun—and to meet nice girls—they played in small area clubs.

A few days after Gloria sang with Emilio's band at the wedding reception, Emilio asked her to join his band as a permanent member. He told her that he had just acquired two new musicians and that the band was growing.

Initially, Gloria was very reluctant. She was planning to attend the University of Miami that year on a partial scholarship to study psychology and communications. She didn't want the distraction of performing in a band. Her main reason for hesitating, however, was her intense shyness. She didn't feel like a performer. She

felt unattractive and overweight. She didn't want to stand in front of a big audience with a flashy band. She didn't think she was what the audience would want to see anyway.

Emilio didn't give up easily. Gradually, he convinced Gloria to take the chance. He promised that the band would not interfere with her schoolwork and that she could quit if she didn't enjoy performing. Besides, Emilio believed that singing in a band might be just what Gloria needed in order to feel better about herself. In a 1996 interview with *People* magazine Emilio explained, "Gloria's eyes were always pointed down back then. She was sad because of her father. The only moments I saw her come alive was when she sang. Her eyes would come alive."

A picturesque city view from Alhambra Granada, Spain. Emilio and his father spent many years in Spain, where Emilio supported them by playing his accordion in a local restaurant.

In spite of time constraints because of her growing involvement with the band, Gloria continued working toward a degree at the University of Miami.

    Gloria's love of music finally won out over her shyness. She decided to accept Emilio's offer, but first she wanted to discuss it with her mother. Gloria's mother agreed that she could join, but she also insisted that Emilio include Gloria's cousin Merci in the band. Families should stick together, she reasoned. Also, Gloria would be safer and less likely to get into trouble if her cousin was with her. Emilio readily agreed.

    With great trepidation, the two cousins went to meet the other band members and audition. The session took place in the garage of Emilio's aunt, where the band usually rehearsed. The band's manager, Carlos Olivia, was quickly impressed, and the two girls were hired.

To her great surprise, Gloria found that she enjoyed performing. It helped her social life, and it got her out of the house at night so she would not have to spend all her free time studying alone in her room. She was slowly becoming a little less serious and a little more daring. Soon she was out every weekend playing with the band and having great fun.

At the same time, Gloria was attending college and working in the evenings as a Spanish-language interpreter for the U.S. Customs Office at Miami International Airport. During the weekends, the band played at parties, weddings, and bar mitzvahs. They even played at some local clubs. The money wasn't great, but the job was fun. The Miami Latin Boys were beginning to gain local attention, thanks to Gloria and Merci. It was very rare for Latino bands to have women members; if they did, the women were usually relegated to background vocals at best. Emilio, however, was giving Gloria lead vocals on some of the band's songs.

Eventually, as the two cousins' roles in the band grew more prominent, it became clear that the band had to change its name. After some thought, one of the members suggested the "Miami Sound Machine." Gloria didn't like the name. She felt that it was too impersonal and suggested that their music was created by a machine. But Emilio thought it was catchy, and so the name stuck. Armed with its female vocalists, the Miami Sound Machine was poised to make history. Before long, the band's name would be on everyone's lips as it soared to success in the pop music scene.

One of many local bands, the Miami Sound Machine created its unique sound by combining salsa music with ballads and disco. Emilio (back row, center) was convinced that Gloria (center) would lead the band to stardom.

4

THE MACHINE TAKES OFF

Before Gloria joined the Miami Latin Boys, the band played only salsa and Top 40 tunes. With Gloria on board, however, the Miami Sound Machine could take advantage of her beautiful voice and her songwriting abilities. The group started adding ballads and other slow-paced songs—along with some disco—to its repertoire. At the same time, Gloria, who was unfamiliar with traditional salsa music, learned the band's standby tunes. The combination of these different musical traditions led the band to develop a unique sound.

From the start, the Miami Sound Machine stood out from other regional groups. Band member Juan Marcos Avila said, "Our sound evolved from trying to please all of the people. Here in Miami, we have Cubans, Anglos, blacks, South Americans. You have to be very versatile." Today, the distinctive musical blend created by the Miami Sound Machine is termed the "Miami sound." Scores of current artists have been influenced by its combination of pop, disco, rock, and traditional Latin rhythm.

Still shy and unsure of herself, Gloria tried to avoid doing lead vocals. She was unhappy with her appearance and knew that only her deep love of music kept her going. She appeared to be content to play maracas and sing background vocals. But Emilio was sure that Gloria should be up front. He persuaded her to sing some of the band's songs alone—at center stage. These were difficult but exciting days for Gloria. Being a member of the Miami Sound Machine was taking up increasing amounts of her time. Had she made the right choice? She wanted to be a psychologist. She didn't want to be in the spotlight.

Gloria recalls that her maternal grandmother, Consuelo García, who lived with the family, had a great impact on her career choice. "I studied psychology, communications, and languages, but she repeatedly told me that I would be happiest doing something I loved," she remembered. "My grandmother told me after I had been accepted [as a band member] that I had probably taken the most important step of my life."

Those early days of performing were not easy for Gloria. She has described one of her first concerts:

> My knees were knocking. I always thought that was just an expression. It literally happens when you are [experiencing] deep, deep fear. You can actually hear the noise of your knees hitting each other louder than you can hear your heart thumping. The people couldn't see my knees, fortunately, because I was wearing a dress, but I felt naked. . . . I had been warned that if they didn't like you, they would throw [things] at you.

Over the course of years working together, Gloria and Emilio fell in love. Initially, Gloria had thought that Emilio was too wild for her. He was four years older and had a reputation as a womanizer. But over time, Gloria saw that Emilio was a kind, sincere man, and that when he flirted, he flirted with everyone—friends, family, and acquaintances alike.

The newly married Gloria and Emilio Estefan smile at well-wishers. Instead of holding a reception after their wedding ceremony, the couple and their guests visited Gloria's father at the hospital.

But this was also the reason why she did not think he was interested in her in a romantic way. She wasn't aware of his feelings toward her until one July day in 1976 when the Miami Sound Machine was performing on a ship to celebrate the nation's bicentennial. During a break in sets, Emilio asked Gloria to join him on the ship's deck to cool down. They stood together and looked out at the ocean. Then Emilio said to her, "You know, if we get married, I'd bet we'd

Gloria and Emilio take one last look back before leaving for their honeymoon in Japan. Emilio warned Gloria that soon all their time would be devoted to making the band succeed and it would be a long while before they could travel for pleasure again.

get along very well." Gloria was shocked. She had no idea that Emilio felt this way about her. That night, they shared their first kiss.

In 1978, Gloria graduated with highest honors from the University of Miami, and that same year, she married Emilio Estefan in a simple ceremony. Although it was a joyous occasion, there was a touch of sadness to the event. The bride's father, José Fajardo, was so weak that he was unable to attend. He had not left the veterans hospital for years. Instead of finding someone else to walk her down the aisle and perform the tradition of giving her away, Gloria decided she would walk down the aisle alone. "No other male figure in my life deserved that honor," she later said.

After the ceremony, the couple did not have a reception. Instead, they went with some family members and the rest of the wedding party to visit Gloria's father in the hospital. José had stopped recognizing his daughter years before, but she believes that on that day he remembered her once again. As she stood at his bedside in her wedding dress, he whispered, "Glorita."

"I was so happy that he saw right through my eyes. Maybe that's why he recognized me," she said. That day, Gloria also realized that her father did not have much longer to live.

After the wedding, the Estefans honeymooned in Japan. Emilio told Gloria that it might be a very long time before they would be able to travel for pleasure again. He strongly believed that their band was about to take off and that all of their future travels would be promotional tours. When they returned from their honeymoon, they worked even harder to earn a national reputation for the band.

Emilio continued to work for Bacardi Imports, where he was promoted many times. He was a rising star within the company. His coworkers liked him and respected his work ethic, which he carried over into promoting the Miami Sound Machine.

Until then the Miami Sound Machine had earned a following in small local clubs and at parties and wedding receptions. One of its specialties was performing at events called "Los Quince," a Latin tradition similar to the American "Sweet 16" party, but given upon a girl's 15th birthday instead. The parties can be very elaborate affairs. Families sometimes spend as much money on Los Quince as they do on weddings. But there was nothing special about performing at Los Quince. Just about every band in the area performed at such events. The Miami Sound Machine may have had a clever name, but it still wasn't very different from scores of other bands trying to make it in Miami.

Emilio didn't settle for that, however. He had big dreams and big plans. In 1977 the group had released its first album, *Live Again/Renacer*, a self-produced and self-financed project that cost a mere $2,000 to make.

The record went nowhere and is no longer available, but one of the songs on the album became popular on Miami's Spanish radio stations and earned some recognition for the band.

But the Miami Sound Machine had a long way to go. Through much hard work and Emilio's relentless promotion, the band finally landed a recording contract with CBS Discos International, the Latino branch of CBS Records. The band cut four Spanish-language albums for the studio in the early 1980s: *Miami Sound Machine* (1980), *Otra Vez* (1981), *Rio* (1983), and *A Toda Maquina* (1984).

The releases didn't earn much coverage in the United States, but in Puerto Rico and in some South American and Central American countries, they were hits. The Miami Sound Machine began touring throughout the Spanish-speaking nations where the band was popular, and before long its songs had reached the top of the music charts in many South American countries. Still, the group was almost completely unknown in the United States. During those days, Gloria has said, the band would play to a stadium of thousands in a Latin American nation and then return to Miami to play at a small wedding reception.

The changes in Gloria and Emilio's work were accompanied by changes in their family. In 1980, Gloria gave birth to the Estefans' first child, a son they named Nayib. Believing that no child is happy with a mother who is unhappy, Gloria decided that it was important for her to continue her career. At the same time she realized that doing so would require great sacrifices and that there would be times when she would have to leave Nayib behind while she was touring and performing. She and Emilio vowed to take the child with them as often as they could and to provide a secure, loving family life for him.

The joy of Nayib's birth was mixed with family

sorrow. That same year, Gloria's father died after years of suffering. Despite their great grief, Gloria and her family felt relief that the man they so loved was no longer in pain.

In 1982, Emilio left his job at Bacardi Imports to focus solely on the band. Although the future of the Miami Sound Machine looked promising, there were some problems among the band members. They were very close friends and had been working together for a long time. Gloria's cousin Merci had even married band member Raul Murciano. The group was like a family—but

The Miami Sound Machine released its first self-produced album, Live Again/Renacer, *in 1977. The album lists Emilio (center) as the band's leader and credits him for percussion. It also acknowledges Gloria (left, sitting) for vocals and guitar.*

its members also had disagreements the way a family might. Some of the players began to resent Emilio's control and the way he was running the band, especially the way he was promoting Gloria above the other members. It seemed she was out in front for almost every song.

Emilio was clearly in love with Gloria, but he also believed that her looks, her voice, and her presence would help the Miami Sound Machine become more popular. The others did not agree. Some began to feel as though Gloria was getting special treatment because she was Emilio's wife. In addition, as part of their recording deal, band members had been given shares in CBS Discos International—but Emilio did not distribute these shares equally. He kept the greatest amount for himself and Gloria.

Tensions grew. Late in 1982 Raul Murciano quit. He told his wife, Merci, that she should make her own decision about whether to stay with the band. A week later Merci quit as well. To this day, Murciano will not speak to the Estefans. Much of the trouble arose from the fact that Emilio wanted to run the band like a business and had been planning to incorporate the group. While that would help it financially, incorporation would also give Emilio almost complete control of the band's future. Many of the original band members disagreed with this plan, and after the Murcianos left, several other musicians also quit.

The situation was not a complete disaster, however. As its members were replaced, the band began developing its unique sound, which would eventually make it one of the most popular groups in America. A new drummer, Enrique García (nicknamed KiKi), had joined the band in the late 1970s. He was a high-intensity person who loved disco. KiKi's influence contributed to the "crossover" sound the band was trying to achieve. Miami Sound Machine was already well known as a Latin band, but it wanted to branch out and appeal to American pop audiences as well.

Creating a crossover sound—even a crossover song—can be very difficult. Record companies generally discourage their artists from doing so unless they feel that the group stands a good chance of succeeding. Promoting an artist is costly to begin with, but introducing a musician to several different types of audiences significantly increases both the cost and the risk of failure. Miami Sound Machine had released three Spanish-language albums for CBS Discos, and the band wanted to try recording songs in English. With KiKi's keen appreciation of disco music, it seemed possible.

While on a flight during a 1980s European tour, KiKi had written a song called "Dr. Beat," a quick tune with a catchy melody line. He tried to translate his English lyrics into Spanish, but they just didn't sound right. This seemed to be the chance the band was looking for, and Emilio approached the record company to see if it would record the song in English. At first CBS

Discos executives said no, but eventually they relented.

The song was released on the 1984 album *Eyes of Innocence* and was on the "B" side (the less popular side) of a single based on the album. But while Spanish-speaking disc jockeys were playing the "A" side of the single, Anglo disc jockeys had discovered the "B" side. "Dr. Beat" quickly became popular in America, and before long it had landed on both the American and European dance charts. It was remixed into a 12-inch disco single, a type of record that was popular in dance clubs at the time. Twelve-inch singles featured extended versions of two songs, one on each side of the disc. Soon you could hear "Dr. Beat" in dance clubs across the United States. At last, the Miami Sound Machine had the crossover hit they had worked for.

Conflicts between the Estefans and other band members brought changes to the Miami Sound Machine in the early 1980s but Gloria and Emilio continued following their vision of what the group should become.

Gloria and Emilio (right) pose with other band members Marcos Avila (left) and KiKi García (second from left) for a publicity shot. Together, the four musicians brought greater success to the Miami Sound Machine, but observers sensed conflict beneath the surface.

5

PROBLEMS
WITH THE BAND

The song "Dr. Beat" may have been a huge dance hit, but the album *Eyes of Innocence* enjoyed only minor success. Realizing that its one English-language song had taken off, the Miami Sound Machine decided to change record labels after the album's release. The band switched from CBS's Discos division to Epic Records, CBS's international rock division. At first Epic was concerned that the Miami Sound Machine was a "one-hit wonder," a term for an artist or group that produces a hit song but then fails to follow up with any more hits. As a result, the new agreement put great pressure on the band to release a full album that would command the attention of America's pop and rock fans.

By now, the band was very different from the original Miami Sound Machine. Emilio had recruited new musicians from the University of Miami's School of Music. In 1985, just a year after the release of *Eyes of Innocence,* the newly constituted band released the album *Primitive Love*. Epic executives needn't have worried. It seemed to most listeners as though this small band with the big sound had come out of nowhere. Suddenly, across the United

States, radio stations were playing singles from the album, and listeners were clamoring for more.

As it turned out, the new album contained the first major hit for the Miami Sound Machine. "Conga" was a fun, catchy dance tune, named after a kind of Latin dance in which participants hold on to each other's waists from behind and form a long line that snakes around obstacles. Traditionally, conga music is played during festive occasions, such as parties, carnivals, and street festivals. The Miami Sound Machine's song was a huge success, both in the dance market and on pop music charts, and it became the first of the group's songs to land on *Billboard*'s charts.

The song's composer, KiKi García, received primary credit for the hit single. He had created a melody that had universal appeal but still retained the rhythms of Latin music. Knowing that most Americans recognized a conga rhythm, he used it as the base of his song. The band had first performed the newly written song in Amsterdam, where the Dutch fans went crazy.

The Cuban-American community of Miami went crazy, too. They loved the new Miami Sound Machine hit, and they were thrilled to see Gloria and Emilio not only enjoying international success but also receiving recognition in the United States.

The band members made great contributions to their community as well. Every year during the second week of March, Little Havana holds a carnival, staged along the length of Calle Ocho. The carnival is filled with Cuban music, food, and art, and the Miami Sound Machine's annual appearance was gradually improving attendance over the years. Organizers once had to beg corporations to provide sponsorship, but now, with the Miami Sound Machine's popularity, the roles were reversed: companies lined up in hopes of earning a spot on the carnival's sponsorship list.

Because the Miami Sound Machine had done so much for the carnival, its organizers wanted to honor the band in some way. So in 1988, they decided to organize an enormous conga line, which would perform to the Miami Sound Machine's newest hit single. They were out to set a record: previously, the longest conga line had been set up in Burlington, Vermont. But during the 1988 carnival in Little Havana that record was demolished. Nearly 120,000 eager participants stretched for three miles down Calle Ocho. The event put Little Havana in *The Guinness Book of World Records*, and the record still stands.

"Falling in Love" is one of many singles from Primitive Love *that convinced executives at Epic that the Miami Sound Machine was much more than a one-hit wonder.*

Despite the outpouring of affection and appreciation from fans, however, Epic executives remained skeptical of the Miami Sound Machine's future success. But over the next few months, they saw that some of the band's other songs from *Primitive Love* were becoming popular hits. For example, "Bad Boy" and "Words Get in the Way" were receiving a great deal of airtime.

"Words Get in the Way" was Gloria's first hit ballad. She had written it after having an argument with Emilio. Even though the two knew that they loved each other very much, Gloria later explained, she realized after the argument that expressing love for someone else was always difficult. Trying to put those feelings into words sometimes doesn't help, and at times it even hurts. Her emotions came through on the vocals, and American pop fans fell in love with the ballad.

Finally, Epic executives began to realize that the Miami Sound Machine was not a one-hit wonder. Instead, the band looked to be a sound investment that would be popular over the long run. *Primitive Love* sold

Taking Emilio's advice and recognizing the trend for performers to be attractive and sexy in music videos, Gloria hired a personal trainer to increase her fitness level. Gloria and her trainer (above) followed a strict routine of running and other exercise.

more than 2 million copies and sparked a 1986 Miami Sound Machine tour with more than 100 concert dates throughout the United States, Central America, Europe, and Japan. Japanese fans seemed especially fond of the group: Gloria noted that they literally jumped out of their seats during performances. Both she and Emilio were surprised and touched by their appreciation.

With *Primitive Love*'s success came money. Not only did record profits soar, but Pepsi-Cola paid huge royalties to the band to use "Conga" in its TV commercials. Following his keen business sense, Emilio invested that money and then set about building a Miami Sound Machine empire. The band also produced songs for two 1986 movies, *Top Gun*, starring Tom Cruise, and *Cobra*, featuring Sylvester Stallone. The Estefans seemed to be on the fast track at last.

Around this time, Emilio also began to search for a more professional sound. He had ideas of what he wanted the band to sound like, and he was impressed with a local group called the Three Jerks (or simply the Jerks). They were being credited with what is now termed the "Miami sound," a mix of disco and salsa. Emilio aimed for a similar eclectic sound, but he extended it by adding Cuban and Afro-Cuban elements. He approached the Jerks first through the band's Cuban drummer, Joséph Galdo, and managed to gain Galdo's assistance on the Miami Sound Machine's next project. Eventually, all the members of the Jerks joined the Miami Sound Machine as studio musicians and producers.

In the meantime, Emilio worked on Gloria's presentation as well. Gently but persistently, he told her that she could improve herself "200 percent." At first, Gloria found his suggestions insulting and took them as indications that he wasn't pleased with her performances. But after a while, she realized he was trying to make a good thing even better, and she took up the challenge. For herself as well as for the band, she began to exercise regularly, and she hired a personal trainer. She lost more than 40 pounds by following a routine of exercise-bike riding and running.

Part of Gloria's inspiration to get in better shape was the new trend that was taking off in the United States—the music video. If Gloria was going to appear on MTV a dozen time a day, she wanted to appear attractive and sexy. She and Emilio realized that in the coming years, whether they liked it or not, a large part of an artist's or band's success would center on appearance.

Before music videos, musicians could produce scores of records, but fans had few opportunities to see what their favorite peformers looked like. The advent of the music video changed all that. Emilio supported his wife in her efforts to lose weight, but not simply for promotional reasons. He also believed that changes in her appearance would help strengthen Gloria's fragile self-esteem. He cheered her on while she lost weight and toned her body, and he encouraged her as she changed her diet to include more fruits, vegetables, and fish.

As the popularity of the Miami Sound Machine grew, the Estefans knew that they could not simply rest on their achievements. To reach the top in American mainstream music, to truly become crossover musicians, they had to work harder than ever. The next few years were a whirlwind of recording, writing music, producing new sounds—and gathering awards. It seemed that nothing could stop or slow down the Miami Sound Machine.

After years of hard work, Gloria achieved unquestioned success and fame. Signing promotion photos (such as the one above) for her millions of fans, living for months on the road, and continuing to push for excellence made her life busier than ever.

6

THE PRICE OF FAME

Because the band had retained so few of its original members, Emilio decided to change its name once again to showcase his wife's central role. The band became Gloria Estefan and the Miami Sound Machine. Emilio himself had quit performing and begun working full-time as the group's producer and promoter. Members of the Jerks helped ensure the success of the next album, *Let It Loose*. Released in 1987, the album sold more than 3 million copies and produced four Top 10 hits.

For Gloria, having Emilio quit the band to devote time to behind-the-scenes work was difficult. She realized that she was on her own from then on during performances, but her confidence was growing. Still, she often wished he would come out on stage with her again.

The new album contained another beautiful ballad written by Gloria called "Anything for You." Gloria had written this song in a few minutes, as she sat in a diner before heading into the recording studio. With very little rehearsal, the song was recorded in one take. Amazingly, it became the band's very first number one hit.

Gloria Estefan enthralls fans in Tokyo, Japan, as part of the band's 20-month worldwide tour that took place from 1987 through 1988.

Let It Loose was the band's biggest hit so far—it remained on the charts for more than two years, and it was as popular in Europe (where it had been released as *Anything for You*) as it was in the United States. To promote the album, Gloria Estefan and the Miami Sound Machine launched a 20-month worldwide tour. It was a grueling period for the traveling musicians, but Gloria in particular never slowed. Band member Joséph Galdo described her as an incredibly hard worker. "[There was] no prima donna groove," he said of the lead vocalist. "If there was something wrong with a track at four in the morning, she'd say, 'Okay, let's work on it.'"

Perhaps it was inevitable that during this stressful time, problems would arise once again among the band members. The original artists who had stayed with the band were resentful of the fact that Emilio had changed its name to Gloria Estefan and the Miami Sound Machine. In 1986, a reporter from *People*

magazine noticed that although Gloria said in an interview that the band members got along well, this didn't
appear to be the case. The Miami Sound Machine was
achieving fame, but the one who was becoming most
recognizable was Gloria. This didn't sit well with some
members, and before long rumors arose in the music
world of a rift growing between the original musicians
and the Estefans.

With all the band's difficulties, however, no one
denied that Gloria's voice and her ballads powered the
band's success. After the tour, KiKi García left the
band, stating that he believed it had become too much
of a production, had strayed too far from simple music-
making, and was being used to promote Gloria herself.
Members of the Jerks remained with Emilio, however,
and in 1988 they were nominated for a Grammy Award
for Best Producer. Despite its problems, the band itself
was triumphant: that same year, Gloria Estefan and the
Miami Sound Machine won the American Music
Award for Best Pop/Rock Group.

Emilio realized that much of the band's success
hinged on the distinctive sound of the Jerks members,
and he tried in vain to sign them on as his exclusive
musical property. This kind of contract would have
prevented the Jerks from performing or recording with
other bands, so they were not interested. They wanted
the freedom to work on other projects of their own
choosing. Angry over what he considered a betrayal,
Emilio told them he no longer needed their services.

The Jerks were also angry. They believed that
Emilio had taken too much credit for the new Miami
sound. They attacked Emilio in the press, accusing
him of trying to control their careers. Joséph Galdo
said that the Miami Sound Machine was a "ridicu-
lously bad band that played open houses, weddings
and little clubs" and that without his help and that of
the other Jerks members, it would still be a bad band.
The musicians claimed that their artistic contributions

had given the band its universal sound and directly caused its success. The Jerks also stated that while they had earned thousands of dollars from the sales of *Primitive Love*, Emilio had earned millions.

The Jerks left and have never since spoken to Emilio, who still maintains that he and Gloria were the ones who made the Miami Sound Machine so successful. While he acknowledges that the musicians they hired over the years contributed to that success, he believes that the band members tried to take too much credit for Gloria's accomplishments. On the other hand, members like KiKi García have said that the Estefans seemed so driven to succeed that they didn't care if they lost friends in the process. Although that may be a result of Emilio's trying to run the band like a business, it seemed to KiKi that the price they paid for that success was too high. He describes the last time he saw the Estefans: "On my last night I asked everybody to sign a band T-shirt, you know, as a souvenir, because I really felt good about having worked with all the guys; they're such great musicians. But when I brought the shirt to Gloria, she got really upset. 'KiKi,' she said, 'you make it sound like we're never gonna see each other again.'" They never did.

There were problems outside the band as well. In 1987 Gloria Estefan and the Miami Sound Machine appeared at the Pan American Games in Chicago. Anti-Castro demonstrators were there in full force, as were Cuban security forces, who were assigned to protect their country's athletes. The producers of the games had asked Gloria to perform at the closing ceremonies and to sing her song "Celebracíon." But many Cuban citizens were unhappy with this choice because Gloria is a Cuban American. They associated her with the anti-Castro demonstrations, and the Cuban athletes threatened to boycott the ceremonies. In the end, when Gloria and the Miami Sound

Machine played to the crowd of more than 40,000, the Cuban athletes were present. But while the rest of the audience danced and cheered, they stayed seated in protest. In response Gloria states that her work is not political and that her music is about love and the joy and sadness it brings.

After KiKi and the Jerks left the band, Emilio set out once again to find replacement musicians. He and Gloria knew exactly the sound they wanted to cultivate for the band, so their search was very direct. He found his band members once again at the University of Miami School of Music, and he also hired new producers. In 1989 the revamped Gloria Estefan and the Miami Sound Machine released the album *Cuts Both Ways*, Gloria having written almost all of the songs. It was an arduous process: "After I write a song," she explained, "the process is so consuming I think I'll never be able to do it again."

Emilio had also decided to make another name change. He dropped "Miami Sound Machine" from the credits on the new album. Instead, it simply stated the artist as Gloria Estefan. For her part, Gloria aimed to increase her recognition around the world, and she recorded many of the music videos for the album both in Spanish and Portuguese (the dominant language of Brazil). *Cuts Both Ways* was a massive success. The album included two hits: the ballad "Don't Wanna Lose You Now" and the rousing "Get on Your Feet." For her efforts, Broadcast Music, Inc. (BMI), a worldwide music agency that sells rights to music, honored Gloria with the 1989 Songwriter of the Year Award.

After the album's release, Gloria, Emilio, and Nayib embarked on the Get on Your Feet Tour, which began in Europe and ended in the United States. Gloria had left Nayib home during the previous tour because he wanted to play on the local Little League baseball team. Being away from her son for long stretches of time was tough for Gloria, and she had vowed not to do it again if she didn't have to. "I was miserable," she recalled. "I was flying home every weekend, and [Nayib and Emilio] were flying out to meet me in different cities. It was really hard on me, and I'm not going to miss out on my kids growing up."

Before the American leg of the tour was over, Gloria began to feel sick. Although she refused to cancel any of the scheduled concerts and tried to perform well, by the time the band reached the Midwest she was clearly very ill. Her voice had gotten so bad that she could only croak out sounds. Gloria tried very hard to continue to perform because she didn't want to disappoint any of her fans. Finally, she agreed to postpone the rest of the tour. Gloria's doctor told her later that she had ruptured blood vessels in her throat, which had caused an infection. It was no wonder she couldn't sing, he said. She was ordered not to speak for two weeks—and not to sing for two full months.

The injury forced Gloria to get some much-needed rest. In January 1990, she reappeared in public when she hosted the American Music Awards ceremony. A short while later, she was nominated for Best Female Vocal Performer in that year's Grammy Awards, and she performed during the awards ceremony. Emilio was also nominated for Best Producer, but neither of them won a Grammy. However, the nominations alone were great honors for them. That March, CBS Records presented Gloria with its Crystal Globe Award, given to those who have sold at least 5 million records outside of their native country. In addition, the band was named the most popular group in the United States by *Billboard* magazine. Energized by the awards and completely healed, Gloria finished her tour through the United States.

Her problems were not over, however. Gloria faced a legal crisis when the song "Oye Mi Canto" from the *Cuts Both Ways* album incited a great controversy. One

of her old friends, the well-respected Latin musician Eddie Palmieri, who had won more than five Grammys, alleged that Gloria had stolen his music to create the tune. Palmieri was recognized as a leader in salsa music; he had led bands and composed music, enjoying most of his fame in the early 1970s before becoming a music producer.

Palmieri believed that Gloria had been inspired by his song "Páginas de Mujer" and that she had stolen some of its melody for "Oye Mi Canto." Gloria could not understand the accusation. Palmieri's music had more of a macho sound, she thought. He sang of the tough life growing up in the barrios (Spanish-speaking neighborhoods) and never created love songs and ballads. In 1991, Palmieri and Sony Music Entertainment filed a $10 million lawsuit (the money they believed Gloria earned through worldwide distribution) against Gloria Estefan in a Manhattan court of law, claiming

Driven to achieve perfection, Gloria, shown working in a recording studio, would stay up as late into the night as necessary to get things right.

Before the 1990 release of Exitos de Gloria Estefan, *Gloria posed for publicity shots to promote the album.*

that "Oye Mi Canto" had been directly taken from "Páginas de Mujer," composed by Palmieri and released in 1981.

Copyright infringement is a very serious charge in the music business. Musicians cannot claim a piece of music as their own unless they have written it themselves; their work must be original. However, sometimes it is hard to separate original music from similar-sounding melodies or riffs that have been inspired by the original song. This is especially difficult to do in cases where the music has been inspired by traditional tunes, such as Latin melodies, that have been incorporated into many pieces that follow that particular sound.

The lawsuit Palmieri launched against Gloria surprised and upset her. To be accused of stealing someone else's music was an awful thing. Gloria claimed that the music from "Oye Mi Canto" was based on a Cuban folk melody. Because these songs have no known origin, they cannot be copyrighted. Gloria claimed that the melody used in her song was inspired by the music she had heard while growing up.

The judge told Palmieri that he had to prove that Gloria had actually heard the song "Páginas de Mujer," and so Palmieri and his lawyers spent a lot of time and money trying to prove that his song was being played by Miami stations when Gloria and Emilio were first starting their band. However, Palmieri could not prove that she had actually heard the song. As a result, the case was dismissed. Gloria was pleased with the verdict, not only because it exonerated her but because she believed that it proved that all artists have a right to use folk melodies in their songs, regardless of whether another musician has also adapted such songs.

Throughout these stormy but successful years, Emilio Estefan expanded his efforts as a producer. He began to work with other artists and promoted his studio tirelessly. As a result, he attracted artists such as Madonna and Clarence Clemons (a former Bruce Springsteen band member). He also began to scout for new talent to produce and promote.

Meanwhile, Gloria and the band were running full-speed ahead. "There's no growth without a lot of hard work and a little risk," Gloria has said. "It's important to me that I continue to grow. There's no point in living life any other way."

Gloria was about to find out how hard she really could work and how great a challenge she could survive. She was also going to learn how much she could grow when faced with overwhelming odds.

JUNE 25, 1990 ■ $1.95

People
weekly

GLORIA ESTEFAN'S
AMAZING
RECOVERY

The Miami Sound Machine star tells the dramatic story of her comeback from the bus accident that broke her back—but not her spirit

On March 20, 1990, an accident on a snowy Pennsylvania road forced Gloria to discover new strength from within.

7

THE ULTIMATE
CHALLENGE

In March 1990, after hosting the American Music Awards and being nominated for a Grammy Award, Gloria received one more honor. President George Bush invited her to Washington, D.C. He wanted to recognize Gloria for her work in sponsoring anti-drug campaigns for children. The invitation marked the pinnacle of the most successful year Gloria and Emilio had yet experienced. "Everything seemed to be going so well for us," Gloria told one reporter. "We were sold out all over. Then we got a call—the President would like to see us." It seemed as though nothing could ruin these fairy-tale days for the Estefans.

After meeting the president, Gloria and Emilio rented a tour bus to take them to New York, where they planned to have dinner with their close friend, musician and vocalist Julio Iglesias. Gloria was feeling tired from all the excitement, and she was looking forward to resting on the bus. The Estefans had brought 10-year-old Nayib, his tutor, and Gloria's personal assistant. In the comfortably accommodated bus—which featured a lounge complete with television, VCR, stereo, and a kitchen full of food—there were many

In March 1990 Gloria met with President George Bush at the White House, where he commended her for the work she was doing in sponsoring campaigns to teach young people about the dangers of drugs.

places to rest. After staying overnight in New York City, the group boarded the bus en route to Syracuse, New York, for Gloria's next performance.

The trip would take them through Pennsylvania's Pocono Mountains. Since it was March, there was a chance of encountering snow in the mountains, but the bus driver was experienced in driving in such weather and in handling the enormous $345,000 bus.

Gloria and Emilio had decided to start taking Nayib on their shorter tours. He loved watching his mother perform and helping the stagehands set up before each concert and break down the sets afterward. Music seemed to be in his blood. He and his tutor were prepared to work on his homework during the bus ride, and then he would be allowed to join the crew in setting up the stage.

Gloria had made sure Nayib was working hard before she settled down to rest with an old detective movie on the VCR. Emilio, always busy, was making business calls on his cell phone at the front end of the bus. Outside, light snow began to fall. Gloria eventually fell asleep as the bus drove into the mountains of Pennsylvania. But the increase in altitude also meant a drop in temperature, and the bus driver began to encounter icy conditions. Here and there, he saw cars that had lost control and skidded off the narrow highway. Gloria slept as the snow fell, and the bus hummed along.

Suddenly the Estefans' driver encountered a traffic jam. A truck in front of the bus had tried to slow down so it wouldn't hit a car being hooked to a tow truck. But the tractor trailer hit a patch of ice and jackknifed, blocking the traffic behind it. Gloria's bus slowed to a stop. The sound of downshifting gears woke Gloria, who looked out the window at the snow and thought about how quiet the scene was and how beautiful everything looked. She wondered why they were stopped, but decided that was the driver's problem.

Earlier that morning, a trucker en route to Toronto, Canada, had left Newark, New Jersey, after picking up a load of dates. His rig was fully loaded, and after having his truck checked for safety, he headed out. He believed that he could make the trip from northern New Jersey to Toronto in about eight hours. He wasn't worried about the snow because he had done this run many times before and was used to the sometimes dangerous driving conditions in the mountains. In addition, he had had a good night's sleep after checking into a motel the day before.

The trucker was speeding along about a half-mile behind Gloria's bus. Two women in a car in front of him saw the jackknifed truck ahead and the cars and tour bus slowing down behind it. They too slowed down. The road was slippery, but they had good visibility and plenty of time to stop. What frightened them was that the driver of the truck behind them looked like he wasn't going to stop. In fact, it seemed like he was going to hit them. To avoid an accident, the woman who was driving steered off the road and onto the median strip.

The truck loaded with dates flew by them. He wasn't stopping, and he seemed to have lost control of the rig. As they watched from the median, the women estimated he was going about 50 miles per hour and that he was trying to avoid disaster by squeezing through a space between the median and the jackknifed truck. He didn't make it. Instead, he smashed directly into Gloria's bus, pushing it into the truck ahead of it.

In an instant, everything changed for Gloria Estefan and her family. "It was like an explosion," Gloria later explained during an interview. There was a terrible sound of tearing metal and breaking glass—and then all was silent. Snow was falling into the bus where the windshield had been. The driver was bleeding. Emilio had flown across the bus, but he felt strong enough to run to the back of the vehicle and check on Gloria and Nayib. He had been knocked out of his shoes by the crash, and his feet were bleeding from the broken glass. But he found Nayib up and moving, rubbing his shoulder; the boy had injured his collarbone. When Emilio got to Gloria, however, it was a different story.

She had landed on the floor of the bus, and she told Emilio that she thought she had broken her back. He assured her that she hadn't, that she had most likely just pulled a muscle, but that she should lie still all the same. Gloria knew differently. She had felt something snap in her back. All of a sudden, she was flooded with terror. She had always been afraid of being dependent on others the way her father had been during his long illness. She had always feared that one day she, too, would be a burden to her family. She thought at that

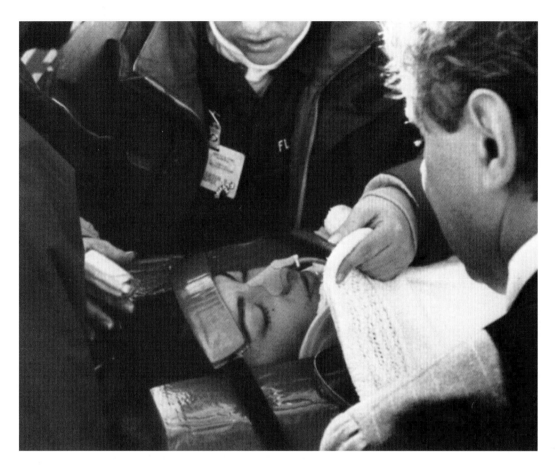

moment that she would rather die than live paralyzed. Overwhelmed with dread, she knew that she was in very bad condition.

Someone pried open the door of the bus, while another person called for help. A nurse who had seen the accident came onto the bus to help. Unsure of how serious Gloria's injuries were, the nurse tried to keep her from moving at all. But it was hard. Gloria was in enormous pain, and medical help was taking a long time to arrive. While she waited, Gloria told herself that she would not accept paralysis. She knew that she had no choice but to hope for the best. She would be fine, she kept telling herself.

Nayib sat with his mother, crying. "I lay flat on my

Placed on a backboard to protect her spine from further injury, Gloria faced excruciating pain and feared her back was broken.

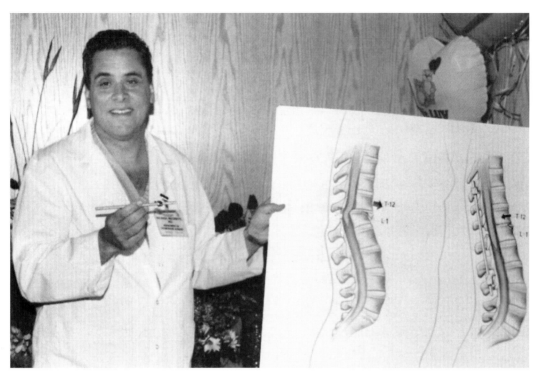

Dr. Michael Neuwirth shows reporters a diagram explaining Gloria's spinal injury. Steel rods like the one he is holding were inserted into her back during surgery to stabilize her spinal column.

back, holding Nayib's hand," Gloria recalled in an interview, "staring at a point on the ceiling. In the back of my mind I couldn't escape the thought: I don't care about money. I don't care about anything except health. It is the only thing I want."

Finally, paramedics arrived, having had to navigate the icy mountain roads themselves. They asked Gloria her name to determine how aware of her surroundings she was. "Oh my," they joked, when she told them. "We have a celebrity here."

Gloria was placed on a backboard that prevented her from moving her back, head, or neck, and she was pulled out of the bus through the broken windshield. The ambulance took her to the Community Medical Center Regional Trauma Center in Scranton, Pennsylvania. The ride to the hospital took nearly an hour. Gloria was in excruciating pain, but she couldn't receive pain-killing medication because the drugs would interfere with the results of tests that doctors wanted to perform upon her arrival. Once she got to the hospital, doctors ran a series of tests, including a CAT scan and X-rays, and then administered pain medicine.

Just as Gloria feared, she had indeed broken her back; she had injured a vertebra, the bone that protects the spinal cord. However, the damage could have been worse: if she had injured her spinal cord, she would have been paralyzed. Gloria's doctors told her she would need to have her spine realigned and that her spinal cord had been pinched, which was causing the severe pain.

At the hospital's nurses station, the phones would not stop ringing. News had leaked out that Gloria Estefan had been injured in an accident, and flowers and messages from fellow celebrities, fans, and even strangers began arriving. Journalists from all over the nation traveled to Pennsylvania to report on the story. Eventually, hospital volunteers were recruited to field phone calls and answer questions about their famous patient's status.

Once Gloria received pain medication and learned that she would not be paralyzed, she felt relieved. Doctors told her that she had two options to correct the injury: she could wear a body cast for six months, or she could undergo an operation. Gloria chose the surgery. Once the situation was clear, Emilio called members of Gloria's family to give them the news. He didn't want them to hear it over the radio or on television. President Bush, whom the Estefans had met just days earlier, called twice to see how Gloria was doing. Floral arrangements continued to pour in, and the Estefans decided to share them by donating many of them to other patients.

Emilio and Nayib, along with Nayib's tutor and Gloria's personal assistant, stayed overnight in Scranton. The day after the accident, they flew by medical helicopter with Gloria to Manhattan's Orthopedic

Institute and Hospital for Joint Disease. As the helicopter lifted off from the roof of the trauma center in Scranton, Emilio noticed a bright patch of sunlight that had fallen on Gloria and him. He quickly wrote on a small piece of paper the phrase that came to him: coming out of the dark. The sunbeam seemed to be a promise that all would work out.

Dr. Michael Neuwirth performed the complex surgery on Gloria without incident. In the three-hour procedure the surgeon inserted two 8-inch steel rods along her spine to stabilize it. The doctor explained that the rods would have to remain in Gloria's back for the rest of her life. The realigned vertebrae were repaired with a piece of bone taken from her hip. While Gloria was under anesthesia, the surgeon also repaired another pinched nerve that had caused the singer trouble for years. The operation left a 14-inch scar down her back, which Gloria did not want to look at for a long time.

Two weeks later, Gloria was ready to go home to Miami. By this time, practically everyone in the United States knew about the accident, and the outpouring of love and good wishes amazed the Estefans. Well-wishers waited for Gloria outside the hospital in New York, at the airport where she boarded the private plane that would carry her home, and at the Miami airport where they landed. In New York, for the first time since her surgery, she had stood up from her wheelchair for a few moments. As the crowd cheered, Gloria cried. When she landed in Miami, however, the crowd was quiet until she had descended from the plane holding onto Nayib's shoulder; then they cheered and cried with her. Miami's favorite daughter was going to be fine. She could walk.

The next few months proved painful and depressing for Gloria. She couldn't avoid seeing her long scar, which made her feel miserable. She had had more than 400 stitches, and they had left their mark. What was even worse was that everything she tried to do caused

great pain. She even feared sneezing because it hurt so much. Gloria could hardly sleep: as the doctors had recommended, Emilio woke her every 45 minutes and helped her take painful steps around the dock of their island home to prevent her muscles from stiffening and becoming sore. "She used to walk and cry at the same time. It was very tough," said Emilio.

But in the agonizingly slow process of recovery, Gloria decided to celebrate the tiniest victories, such as being able to put on her own socks for the first time. As the weeks passed, she realized more and more that she had a great deal to be thankful for. Most important, she hadn't lost her independence.

Gloria smiles to onlookers as she leaves New York's Hospital for Joint Diseases on April 4, 1990, following successful back surgery.

For the next several months, Gloria endured what seemed like countless hours of rehabilitation excercises with her personal trainer. At first her physical therapy consisted of swimming because it strengthened her muscles without putting weight on her back and other parts of her body. Next she moved to more strenuous exercises: lifting weights and eventually running, which was very difficult and painful. But Gloria saw that the harder she worked, the more progress she made. She was determined to recover as fully as possible, with as little loss of muscle as possible. Although her arms and legs had weakened during the recovery period, her trainer told her that she would one day gain all of her strength back—and more.

Gloria's view of life changed drastically while she recuperated from her accident. She no longer worried about trivial problems, and she realized that after she fully recovered many things were going to change. "Because I had studied psychology, I understand the stages [of dealing with a trauma]," Gloria said in 1998. "You have to go through the depression, the crying. Then, at a certain point, I pulled myself up and said 'Okay, no more. You can't continue this way.'" What impressed Gloria most about her situation was not only the heartfelt love of her family and friends, but also the outpouring of sympathy and support from her fans. She will never get over this, she has said; she could actually physically feel this love.

Gloria established a routine of setting small goals and trying to meet them. At last, she finally felt ready to return to the recording studio. And she started to write music again. That was when Emilio showed her the scrap of paper on which he had written the words "coming out of the dark." He explained when he had written the phrase and what caused him to think of it. Gloria sat down and wrote a song for the words in just minutes. The music seemed to come very easily.

Emilio and Gloria Estefan later filed a lawsuit against

some of the people and companies they believed responsible for the accident. The case was tried in Scranton, Pennsylvania, where the police who handled the accident and most of the witnesses lived. In the end, the trial showed that the truck that hit the Estefans' tour bus had brake problems, which explained why witnesses said it seemed to be speeding up in the moments before it collided with the bus. The truck driver testified that even though he applied the brakes, the truck didn't seem to respond, so he tried to steer into the median and avoid hitting other drivers. Even so, the truck was already out of his control. The Estefans won the lawsuit and received an $8.3 million award.

Many of those involved in the suit, including the defendants, later said that the Estefans were wonderfully kind during the trial. Emilio one time offered to buy dinner for the defense attorneys when they traveled to Miami to interview him (they did not accept). Those who met Gloria in Scranton said that she was thoughtful and down-to-earth. At the end of the trial, she signed autographs for fans, and then she and Emilio gave their award money to Scranton's Ronald McDonald House, which provided Emilio and Nayib with a place to stay immediately after the accident.

Although Gloria's speedy recovery appeared miraculous to some, the artist had endured months of grueling workouts and pain to return to normal. By January 1991, she was back on stage to present the American Music Awards, where she received a standing ovation from the audience. Soon afterward she began to record her album *Into the Light,* (the title was based on the phrase Emilio wrote and the song Gloria produced from it), and she and Emilio organized the Coming out of the Dark Tour, which traveled through more than 10 countries. At Gloria's dress rehearsal for the Miami concert, she appeared on stage in a flashy blue-sequined dress and belted "Get on Your Feet"—while dancing. The crowd couldn't stop cheering. Gloria could dance again!

Having experienced suffering herself, Gloria is determined to fight for those in need. Here she hugs a stuffed toy cat donated for people who survived Hurricane Andrew, which struck Florida in 1992. Gloria and Emilio raised millions of dollars to aid hurricane victims.

8

FIGHTING FOR OTHERS

Perhaps Gloria's brush with tragedy intensified her concern for people who had endured traumatic situations. She continued her charity work as wholeheartedly after her accident as she had before. When Hurricane Andrew hit Miami in 1992, Gloria and Emilio, who had escaped injury or property loss, organized a relief concert and raised millions of dollars to aid the victims. The concert not only provided the people of Florida with funds but also raised their spirits.

As a result of her efforts, Gloria was recognized as Humanitarian of the Year by B'nai B'rith, an international Jewish organization. President Bush remained a big fan, seeing in Gloria a positive role model for American children. In 1992, the president appointed her as a representative of the U.S. delegation to the United Nations (UN). Although this honor had been bestowed on many other celebrities, no one responded to it quite like Gloria. She took her new appointment very seriously, and she worked hard to represent U.S. views at the UN. Her first speech in that capacity was before the Commission on Crime Prevention and Criminal Control, but most of her work was done with the United Nations High Commission on Refugees, a cause dear to her heart. She convinced the UN to increase its budget for helping victims of wars and persecution, especially those in northern Africa. She did exchange a few choice words with one of Cuba's delegates, however, and although the conversation was not recorded, reports stated that it was memorable.

If anything, Gloria's accident and her courageous recovery introduced even more fans to her music. In 1992 she released her *Greatest Hits* album, which went platinum (a million copies were sold). She also received a star on the Hollywood Walk of Fame, performed at the halftime show at Super Bowl XXVI as fans danced in the aisles, and sang at the Winter Olympics.

During the 1990s Gloria's music began to change. She drifted closer to her Cuban roots, and she told Emilio that she wanted to release an all-Spanish album. The result was *Mi Tierra*, a beautiful collection of new songs with the flavor of Cuban music from the 1930s and 1940s. The album received great critical acclaim.

Mi Tierra was especially important to Gloria because many guest musicians performed with her, and their work enhanced the project. "The pride I feel over the success of *Mi Tierra* is beyond words," Gloria said. "It's an honor and a thrill to know that music that is purely from the heart and soul was received so well by so many people."

Gloria's goal had been to introduce the music of her home country to her fans around the world, and album sales of more than 4 million showed that she had done just that. *Mi Tierra* went platinum in the United States, and any concerns about being able to market an all-Spanish album vanished when the project earned a 1994 Grammy for Best Tropical Latin Album—Gloria's first Grammy. The musician also received an honorary doctorate of music from her alma mater, the University of Miami.

Flush with the success of Gloria's newest album, she

In 1992, President George Bush appointed Gloria as a representative of the U.S. delegation to the United Nations. She convinced the UN officials of the need to spend more money to aid refugees throughout the world.

Gloria received a star on the Hollywood Walk of Fame in 1992, the same year that she performed at the halftime show at Super Bowl XXVI and sang at the Winter Olympics.

and Emilio soon welcomed another child into their family. Emily Marie Estefan was born on December 5, 1994. The birth went smoothly—despite the fact that Emilio fainted while keeping Gloria company in the delivery room. He was wheeled out of the room but returned a few minutes later to cut his new daughter's umbilical cord. The couple chose musician Quincy Jones as Emily's godfather, and they brought the little girl home. Today, Emily accompanies her mother just about everywhere; Gloria claims that Emily aspires to be a singer like her mother someday.

The year after Emily's birth, Gloria released another Spanish album titled *Abriendo Puertas*. She followed it up with two minor albums: a holiday album called *Christmas Through Your Eyes* and a conventional English-language album, *Hold Me, Thrill Me, Kiss Me*.

Abriendo Puertas was poorly received. Gloria intended the music on the album to incorporate the influences of Colombia, Panama, the Dominican Republic, and Cuba. But many people believed that her vocals were overpowered by the strong dance rhythms. Though the album sold poorly, it earned Gloria a second Grammy for Best Tropical Latin Performance. The songs from this record remain favorites in Gloria's international concert appearances, where they bring most audiences to their feet within seconds of hearing the opening notes.

But the Estefans were in for more heartache in 1995, when they left their home one day in early fall for a pleasure cruise along Miami Beach. Their house is on Star Island, which sits in Biscayne Bay near Miami. On pleasant days, the bay is filled with boaters and "wet bikers" (people riding on Jet Skis and Wave Runners). On September 24 Gloria and Emilio packed a lunch and set out for a long boat ride. Vacationers waved and called to them from tour boats as they recognized the famous couple cruising through the waters.

A few hours later Gloria and Emilio arrived at the mouth of the bay and then headed out toward the Atlantic Ocean. Then they decided to return home and began heading back. At the same time Maynard Howard Clarke, a 29-year-old law student at Howard University, and his girlfriend were on the bay riding on a rented Wave Runner. At the helm of his own 33-foot motorboat, Emilio saw the young man approaching and was puzzled because Clarke didn't appear to be steering away from him. The Wave Runner made it past the bow of the Estefans' boat, but then it crashed into the side.

The Estefans reacted quickly to the accident. Emilio jumped into the water and pulled the two riders into his boat. "Emilio was brave," Gloria proudly related. But Emilio didn't feel so courageous. "I was worried about barracudas and sharks. There was blood all over the place, and I'm thinking my legs are going to be eaten in front of my wife."

Maynard Clarke had been pulled under the boat and cut by the engine's sharp-edged propellers around his shoulders and throat. He died before Emilio and other rescuers could get him to a hospital. His girlfriend escaped without injury.

Emilio and Gloria were stunned, but no longer required at the scene of the accident, they realized they needed to act clearly and quickly to make sure that later they would not be blamed for what happened. Emilio drove to the local Coast Guard station and asked to be tested immediately for alcohol and drug use. He had been drinking only water, and he wanted to be sure that any possible suspicions about his navigating abilities did not cloud the accident investigation. No criminal charges were filed against the couple, but the experience left both Gloria and Emilio very saddened. Gloria called Clarke's parents to talk to them about their son and his last moments. To this day, she says that call was the hardest thing she has ever had to do, but the family was extremely appreciative and was touched by her kindness and concern.

Emilio later speculated that Clarke had been trying to "jump the wake," a risky practice in which a personal watercraft operator rides on the wake of a passing motorboat. The water's turbulence often makes the smaller craft become airborne for several seconds—a thrill sought by many, but an extremely dangerous maneuver.

As a result of the accident, Emilio and Gloria went on a crusade to change Florida's lax boating laws. For years, many other people had requested that the state impose tighter restrictions, but since tourism is one of Florida's biggest industries, it was feared that such changes would reduce its appeal as a vacation destination. Gloria and Emilio went to the state capital, Tallahassee, to speak to the legislature about the need

Gloria loves boating, but the Estefans' involvement in a tragic accident in 1995 moved both Gloria and Emilio to persuade Florida's legislators to change the state's boating education laws.

for changing Florida's boating laws. Their celebrity status, their tragic experience with Maynard Clarke, and their eloquence helped convince lawmakers that boating education laws should be enacted. Many of the politicians who spoke and worked with the Estefans were impressed by their conviction and sincerity. Laws that probably wouldn't have been passed otherwise are in effect today in Florida because of Maynard Clarke and the Estefans. Gloria has said that while she never wanted to restrict freedoms, she also didn't want anyone to have to deal with a similar situation, which could have been prevented if stricter laws had been in place.

The enthusiasm with which Gloria approaches her performances, including the above 1996 Miami concert, marks every other area of her life as well.

9

A TRUE WOMAN OF ACHIEVEMENT

For the little Cuban girl who grew up in poverty, the 1990s brought a great deal of success. Gloria attributes her current good fortune to positive thinking. Her background in psychology allows her to see how much of what happens to people is under their control. While Gloria Estefan's career is no longer as fast-paced as it was before Emily's birth, she is still going strong. In 1996, she released the popular and catchy album *Destiny* and performed the inspiring song "Reach" at the Summer Olympics in Atlanta, Georgia. The song became the theme of the Summer Games.

Two years later, she released *gloria!* to much critical acclaim, and in 1999 she appeared in her first feature film, a movie called *Music of the Heart*, starring Meryl Streep as a tough but caring music teacher for underprivileged children. The new millennium began with an extended world tour for Gloria: "While I still have the energy, I better do it," she said. "I want to stay home when Emily starts school. Not to retire—but it will be much longer between this and the next tour." She also released the album *Alma Caribeña* in 2000.

Gloria hopes that the next phase of her life allows her to spend plenty of time with her family. Even her hard-driving husband, Emilio, admits that they have accomplished a great deal and that they now have time to relax, make the music they want to make, and have fun, without worrying about commercial success or critical praise. In fact, Gloria's desire to try acting was inspired by 5-year-old Emily. By landing more acting parts Gloria hopes to have more time to stay home with her children than concert tours have allowed. But she also wants to "spread her wings" as an artist. "It is another daunting mountain to climb, and it's one that I'm looking forward to," Gloria explained.

To that end, Gloria has been taking acting lessons, and she received strong reviews for her performance in *Music of the Heart*. Gloria feels it is important for her to start out with small roles first to get used to the craft. She auditioned for and won the role of Eva Peron in the movie version of *Evita*, but then decided not to take it, saying that the role gave her a "too-much-too-soon feeling." (Pop singer and actress Madonna played the part instead.) "I want to start small, no pressure," Gloria stated. "I want to do it slow and well. I wouldn't want to star in my first film, wouldn't want the pressure of carrying it. . . . Right now I want strong actors around me to pull people in."

Gloria enjoys being at home with her active family. Emily is still small, but Nayib has grown into a handsome college student with a love for practical jokes—and with a bit of a wild streak. He was asked to leave Miami's Gulliver Prep School because he called a fellow student's home and imitated the school's principal, telling the student's mother that her son was to be expelled. The mother had the call traced to the Estefan home and discovered the call had been made by Nayib. As a result, Gloria had him quit his garage band (which he calls Psychosis), and Emilio made him join the construction crew that was putting additions on their house. For five weeks, Nayib

The more professional success Gloria achieves, the greater the financial investment that is placed in her projects. This sign is one of many promotional tools used to advertise her 1998 release, gloria!

woke at 5:00 A.M. and worked all day in the tropical sun.

While the Estefans believe in disciplining their children, they also allow Nayib many freedoms. "[Nayib] wants more freedom than he can handle. We'll give him freedom when he shows that he is responsible," said Gloria. Recently Nayib was grounded for neglecting to shut a door and allowing the Estefans' five Dalmatians (Lucy, Ricky, Red, Tiny, and Holly) to escape. Emilio complained that he had to look for the dogs at four

Gloria is exploring a future in acting, in part because she believes it would allow her to spend more time with her family. Her first movie role was in Music of the Heart, *a 1999 film starring Meryl Streep (center) and Angela Bassett (right).*

o'clock in the morning while Nayib slept.

Emilio says that his son is a good kid who has to learn from his mistakes. Gloria sees ways in which Nayib is just like his father. "These two are pranksters, the kind that hide behind walls to scare you. Neither one has ever experienced a day of shyness," she exclaimed. In fact, both Emilio and Nayib have scared many maids almost to death with their practical jokes.

Gloria has also said that raising a son properly has

been a huge challenge. "Latin women tend to raise men who are big babies. They think that you have to do everything for them and that they are the king of the house. I've been trying to counteract that my whole life. I've tried to instill in [Nayib] a respect for women. I tell him to just be honest. You can be anything you want as long as you are upfront." As her rowdy but well-meaning son begins college and looks forward to his own musical career, it looks as though she has succeeded admirably.

On the other hand, Emily is a miniature version of her mother. She is shy, and she sometimes tries to hide from people when they are looking at her. Mother and daughter are extremely close, and Emily may also be a budding musician. "Each morning I start sipping my Cuban coffee," Gloria explained, "and Emily and I laugh and play and sing. Emily loves music. Her personality is just like mine." Emily and Gloria can always be found together on the grounds of the family's Star Island estate. "I come here every afternoon with Emily. She loves being outside and is always looking for lizards and worms. I would love to plant a garden for her."

A garden for Emily may be on the agenda, but for now it will have to wait. On a typical day, Gloria said, "I get up in the morning around 10, have two cups of coffee (at least). . . . My husband is up at the crack of dawn and has already checked on business." Gloria stays up late many nights working on songwriting—a quiet time for her, when the rest of the family is sleeping and she can concentrate. She describes herself as a night owl. Some days aren't easy though, especially when she is planning a tour or working on an album. Then she appears on talk shows, gives interviews for the media, and spends hours in photo shoots.

But Gloria remains down-to-earth. She has retained her two lifetime best friends as her employees: Patty Escoto, her friend from Our Lady of Lourdes High School, is the assistant to Emilio and Estefan Productions, and Becky Fajardo, Gloria's sister, assists in planning tours and handling the media. Becky jokes that it is tough to work with Gloria sometimes because her famous sister has such a saintly image and has been described by many columnists as an angel and a great role model. After Gloria's accident, Becky began answering the phones with the phrase "Our Lady of the Rods," poking gentle fun at Gloria and her back surgery.

But Gloria doesn't mind the jokes. One of her greatest assets is her ability to laugh at herself. Fans and the media may see her as angelic, but she does not take herself so seriously:

> I hope to God people don't think I'm a saint. Maternal? Yes. Saintly? No. A saint isn't real. It's an image, not a person, but it's easiest for the media to focus on a generality instead of something multidimensional. It's easiest to exaggerate my sainthood, and make me only "Miami Nice." I'm sure [flamboyant basketball star] Dennis Rodman has a very quiet reflective side but we never see that. . . . Look though, I have a toe ring. Puts me closer to Dennis Rodman than you thought, huh?

Both Gloria and Emilio realize their lives are very rich in many ways. Gloria has loved her career, and she loves her fans. "I consider myself lucky to be able to make a living off something I love to do," she declared. She's said that entering her 40s has brought her peace within herself and with her life. Many times she is contemplative and serene—in contrast to her ever-busy husband, who never seems to rest. She explains, "I love the end of the day, when I feel accomplished and somewhat relieved, and Emilio loves the beginning because he thinks of how much he can't wait to accomplish."

Perhaps Gloria's biggest strength is her positive outlook, which, whether she wants it or not, makes her a great role model. "If you have a dream, don't let anything get in your way," Gloria tells women and girls, and having gone through so many trials

she may have the right to say these words. "All my life, I had three big fears that consumed me—that I would end up in a wheelchair, that I would have a terrible accident on the tour bus and that we'd hit somebody with our boat. All three things happened. So you tell me. I think we have the power to make positive things happen in our lives. We just can't put negative things out there."

"I want to inspire people to move beyond the darkness, empower them," declared Gloria Estefan, ever positive. She has done that—and much more.

Gloria announces the details of her Millennium Concert Spectacular that was held on New Year's Eve 1999 in Miami, Florida.

CHRONOLOGY

1957   Gloria Maria is born to the Fajardos in Havana, Cuba, on September 1

1959   Fidel Castro overthrows the Cuban government and moves into power; Gloria and her family flee to Miami

1961   Gloria's father, José Fajardo, is captured during the Bay of Pigs invasion and is imprisoned in Cuba

1962   José Fajardo is released from prison and returns home to Miami

1974   Emilio Estefan starts a singing group called the Miami Latin Boys

1975   Gloria meets Emilio and joins his band

1976   Emilio renames the band the Miami Sound Machine (MSM)

1977   MSM releases its first self-produced album, *Live Again/Renacer*

1978   Gloria graduates from the University of Miami; marries Emilio

1980   Gives birth to a son, Nayib

1980–84   MSM releases four Spanish-language albums for CBS Discos International, which achieve modest success in Latin American countries

1984   *Eyes of Innocence*, MSM's first English-language album, is released

1985   *Primitive Love*, featuring the hit song "Conga," is released by MSM

1986   MSM wins three American Music Awards for Top New Pop Artist, Top Pop Singles Artist, and Top Adult Contemporary Single ("Can't Stay Away from You")

1987   *Let It Loose* is released

1988   MSM wins an American Music Award for Best Pop/Rock Group

1989   Gloria's first solo album, *Cuts Both Ways*, is released; wins Broadcast Music, Inc. (BMI) Songwriter of the Year award

1990   Breaks her back in a bus accident but makes full recovery

1991   Releases *Into the Light*; kicks off a world tour

1992   Is appointed as a public member of the U.S. delegation to the 47th General Assembly of the United Nations

1993   Receives an honorary doctorate in music from the University of Miami; receives a star on the Hollywood Walk of Fame; *Mi Tierra* is released

1994   Receives her first Grammy Award for *Mi Tierra*; daughter, Emily Estefan, is born

1995   *Abriendo Puertas* is released

1996   Wins her second Grammy for Best Tropical Latin Performance for *Abriendo Puertas;* releases the album *Destiny;* the single "Reach" becomes the official anthem of the 1996 Summer Olympics in Atlanta, Georgia; performs the song at the Olympics closing ceremonies

1998   Releases *gloria!*

1999   Makes her feature-film debut in *Music of the Heart,* starring Meryl Streep

2000   Receives Award of Merit honor at the American Music Awards; *Alma Carbena* is released

DISCOGRAPHY

Albums

1977   *Live Again/Renacer* (Miami Sound Machine)

1979   *Miami Sound Machine: Imported* (Miami Sound Machine)

1980   *Miami Sound Machine* (Miami Sound Machine)

1981   *Otra Vez* (Miami Sound Machine)

1982   *Rio* (Miami Sound Machine)

1983   *Lo Mejor de MSM* (Miami Sound Machine)
       7-Up Presenta Los Hits de Miami Sound Machine
          (Miami Sound Machine)

1984   *A Toda Maquina* (Miami Sound Machine)
       Eyes of Innocence (Miami Sound Machine)

1985   *Primitive Love* (Miami Sound Machine)

1987   *Let It Loose* (Gloria Estefan & MSM, 1987)

1989   *Cuts Both Ways* (Gloria Estefan & MSM, 1989)

1990   *Exitos de Gloria Estefan*

1991   *Into the Light*

1992   *Greatest Hits*

1993   *Mi Tierra*
       Christmas Through Your Eyes

1994   *Hold Me, Thrill Me, Kiss Me*

1995   *Abriendo Puertas*

1996   *Destiny*

1998   *gloria!*

2000   *Alma Caribena—Caribbean Soul*

Hit Singles in the United States

From *Primitive Love*
>"Bad Boy"
>"Conga"
>"Falling in Love (Uh-Oh)"
>"Words Get in the Way"

From *Let It Loose*
>"Anything for You"
>"Betcha Say That"
>"Can't Stay Away from You"
>"Rhythm Is Gonna Get You"
>"1-2-3"

From *Cuts Both Ways*
>"Don't Want to Lose You"
>"Get on Your Feet"
>"Here We Are"

From *Into the Light*
>"Coming Out of the Dark"
>"Live for Loving You"

From *Hold Me, Thrill Me, Kiss Me*
>"Everlasting Love"
>"Turn the Beat Around"

AWARDS

1986   Three American Music Awards; first prize from Annual Tokyo Music Fair for "Conga" (MSM)

1987   American Music Award (MSM)

1988   *Performance* Magazine Reader's Poll Award, Female Vocalist of the Year; American Music Award for Best Pop/Rock Group; BMI Songwriter of the Year Award

1989   *Billboard* Award for Songwriter of the Year

1990   MTV Video Music Award for "Oye Mi Canto"

1991   Movieland Star Hall of Fame; BMI Songwriter of the Year; *Billboard* Music Video Award for Best Latin Female Artist

1992   Humanitarian of the Year; *Premio Lo Nuestro* Lifetime Achievement Award

1993   Hispanic Heritage Award; United Way Outstanding Philanthropy from Alexis de Tocqueville Society; Star on the Hollywood Walk of Fame; Sculpture in Madame Tussaud's Rock Circus Exhibition

1994   Grammy Award for Best Latin Tropical Album for *Mi Tierra*; Musicares Person of the Year

1995   *Billboard* Music Video of the Year for "Everlasting Love"

1996   Grammy Award for Best Latin Tropical Album for *Abriendo Puertas*

1997   Accepted in the Songwriter Hall of Fame; BMI Prestigious President's Award to both Gloria and Emilio

1999   ALMA Lifetime Achievement Award

2000   Award of Merit from American Music Awards; Latin Grammy Award for Best Music Video for "No Me Dejes de Querer"

Books and Periodicals

Castro, Peter. "Little Glorita: Happy at Last." *People*, 12 August 1996.

Catalano, Grace. *Gloria Estefan*. New York: St. Martin's Press, 1991.

Clarke, Anne Patrice. *Gloria Estefan . . . Just Like Any Other Family.*
    Dakini 1, no. 1.

Davis, Patty. "Life in Tune." *Living Fit*, April 1998.

De Stefano, Anthony. *Gloria Estefan*. New York: Signet Publishers, 1997.

Drummond, Tammerlin. "Turning the Beat Around." *Time*,
    20 October 1997.

"Gloria Estefan." *Parents*, March 1998.

Goldsmith, Sarah. "Gloria in Excelsis." *In Style*, October 1996.

Gonzales, Fernando. *Gloria Estefan: Cuban American Singing Star*.
    Brookfield, Conn.: Millbrook Press, 1993.

Le Batard, Dan. "A Blaze of Gloria." *New Woman*, December 1997.

Martin, Lydia. "Gloria Estefan." *Latina Magazine*, December 1997.

McLane, Daisann. "The Power and the Gloria," *Rolling Stone*,
    June 14, 1990.

Padgett, Tim. "Tough as Males." *Time*, 3 August 1998.

Roberts, John S. *The Latin Tiger: The Impact of Latin American Music on
    the United States*. New York: Oxford University Press, 1979.

Shirley, David. *Gloria Estefan: Entertainer*. Philadelphia: Chelsea House
    Publishers, 1994.

Stefoff, Rebecca. *Gloria Estefan*. Hispanics of Achievement. Philadelphia:
    Chelsea House Publishers, 1999.

BIBLIOGRAPHY

Websites

AltoCelebs
www.altocelebs.com/e/gloria-estefan

DIVAstation
www.divastation.com/gloria_estefan/estefan_bio.html

Estefan Online
www.estefan.com

gloria! Estefan U.K. Fan Club
www.gloria.ndirect.co.uk

Gloria Estefan
www.gloriaonline.com

Gloria Estefan & the Miami Sound Machine (unofficial)
www.almetco.com/estfan/musician.html

Mr. Showbiz
http://mrshowbiz.go.com/people/gloriaestefan/index.html

INDEX

PICTURE CREDITS

Jane Phillips is a big fan of Latin music (she was "salsa" when salsa wasn't cool) and a great admirer of Gloria Estefan. Phillips lives in Pittsburgh, Pennsylvania, where she dreams of warm, sunny climates and lots of conga beats.

Matina S. Horner was president of Radcliffe College and associate professor of psychology and social relations at Harvard University. She is best known for her studies of women's motivation, achievement, and personality development. Dr. Horner has served on several national boards and advisory councils, including those of the National Science Foundation, Time Inc., and the Women's Research and Education Institute. She earned her B.A. from Bryn Mawr College and her Ph.D. from the University of Michigan, and holds honorary degrees from many colleges and universities, including Mount Holyoke, Smith, Tufts, and the University of Pennsylvania.